The Spirit of Pong

by

Larry Hodges

Copyright ©2015
v07-03-15

Cover Illustration by Mike Mezyan of Mezyantt.com

<u>Bonus Short Story at End</u>
Ping-Pong Ambition

The Spirit of Pong

Dedication

*To table tennis players everywhere.
Especially the spirited ones.*

The Spirit of Pong

Introduction

This story was many years in the almost-making. I'm a professional table tennis coach & writer, and a professional science fiction & fantasy writer. What could be more natural than combining these two? Just about anything else.

Let's face it. Most stories about table tennis use the sport as a punch line. How could anyone take ping-pong seriously? But how about the Olympic Sport of Table Tennis? They really are the same thing, and you can call it either one. I actually like the stories that make fun of the sport! Those who know our sport know better. Those who don't—well, why not take a quick trip to www.youtube.com, search for "Olympic Table Tennis," and see what comes up?

I've always wanted to combine the two, but it's not easy finding a mix. I did write and sell "Ping-Pong Ambition," the bonus short story at the end of this book. But I wanted something more serious. And then, one day, I mused over the idea of an American going to China to learn the secrets of table tennis . . . and this story was the result. This is not a conventional story, this is a fantasy. You will meet the spirits of a number of the past greats of our sport, and even the spirits of "what made them great" for some current and living players. (Be forewarned—some of the following contain minor spoilers.)

All of the spirits that appear are, or were, real players. Much research went into the three main spirits (Ichiro Ogimura, Rong Guotuan, and the one I've nicknamed the "Dragon," but won't name here), and other aspects of the story. As normally happens in this situation, only a fraction of what I learned could actually be used or it would come off as an encyclopedia. I encourage you to Google or Wiki the various names. The only ones that are made up are the current Chinese team members and head coach, the current U.S. Champion and U.S. Coach, and the two main characters, Andy "Shoes" Blue and Coach Wang. The U.S. Champion is named after three of the top up-and-coming players at my club, Derek Nie, Klaus Wood, and Nathan Hsu (and his older brother, now a coach, John). The U.S. Coach is named after Dan Seemiller and Stefan Feth, both of whom

The Spirit of Pong

coached the U.S. Men's Team at the Worlds. (He's also named after Daniel Sofer, a student of mine who's one of the best ten-year-olds in the country, who found three typos. Nathan Hsu also found a few.) And of course the Chinese head coach in the story, Kong Guoliang, is a combination of the Chinese superstar players and coaches, Kong Linghui and Liu Guoliang.

Most of the training exercises, quotes, and cultural items in the Ogimura section are for real. He was a fan of Van Gogh and Louis Armstrong, enjoyed rice balls wrapped in seaweed and Old Parr Scotch Whisky, and at annual parties sang *Danny Boy*. The faded violet shirt, originally much darker, was given to him by Hisae Uehara, who ran the club where he trained and often took care of him. The quotes about an airplane propeller, dilly-dallying, worms, extraordinary effort, launching a serve, setting a personal best each day, and having the guts to sing in front of others are all real. So are many of the training exercises. The description of him as "Mr. Miyagi" came from Stellan Bengtsson.

I had to use a little more literary license in the Rong Guotuan segment, but the basic facts about his tragic story during the Cultural Revolution are for real.

I also used a number of real-life experiences in the book. For example, in chapter five the part about a player giving away a fast serve by sticking out his tongue is real—I coached a number of times against a former U.S. team member who did this, and he never did figure out why his fast, deep serves never caught my students off guard!

If you are a player yourself, I hope this story inspires you to higher levels. You might also enjoy the inside table tennis, even if embedded in a fantasy story. But player or not, I hope you'll enjoy this fantasy story of an American table tennis player trying to learn the secrets of table tennis in China, the center of table tennis on this planet.

Acknowledgements

A lot of people helped with this book. Without them, it wouldn't have been possible. Special thanks go to:
- The *Great Eight*, who critiqued early versions of this story. **Honfai Geoffrey Cheng, Chris Grace, Vince Green, Nathan Hsu, Navin Kumar, John Olsen, Raul Rasay,** and **Dennis Taylor**.
- **Stellan Bengtsson**, who spent an hour on the phone telling me about his 3.5 months training with Ichiro Ogimura in 1969-1970.
- **Tim Boggan**, USATT Historian.
- **Etsuko Enami**, ITTF Project Manager, who personally sent me the English version of the Ogimura book, which wasn't available in the U.S.
- **Ariel Chen** and **Qihong Cui** from Mytabletennis.net, who helped with some research.
- **Mike Mezyan**, who created the cover.
- **Ledo's Pizza, Hong Kong Café**, and the back room of the **Maryland Table Tennis Center**, three places where I got a lot of work done, ate a lot of pizza and Kung Pao Chicken, and played a little ping-pong.
- And all the **Champions** whose spirits appear in this book!

I owe a lot of thanks to the following four books:
- **Ogi: The Life of Ichiro Ogimura,** by Mitsuru Jojima, translated by John Senior (2009).
- **Ping-Pong Diplomacy: The Secret History Behind the Game That Changed the World,** by Nicholas Griffin (2014).
- **Table Tennis Legends,** by Zdenko Uzorinac and ITTF (2001).
- **The Ogimura Seminar of Table Tennis,** by Dell Sweeris (1968).

Chapter 1
China

Call me loser.

I had searched for the great whale for many years. Only the whale I sought was table tennis glory. I want to be the best. The World Champion. When I walk down the street, I want people to point at me and say, "There goes the greatest table tennis player who ever lived." And so I trained, hour after hour, week after week, year after year, until my feet were callused husks. If the coach said run five miles, I'd do ten. If he said do footwork drills for half an hour, I'd do an hour. If he said practice serves for an hour, I'll do two.

I was Andy "Shoes" Blue, the hardest working player in America. They called me "Shoes" because I wore them out so fast. And yet, just a few weeks ago in December, for the third straight year, I'd lost in the quarterfinals of men's singles at the USA Nationals. I was 25, and no longer the wunderkind I'd been as a junior. It's been a month, but I still wake up every morning with burning tears in my eyes, seeing that last power shot zip past me, just out of reach, and seeing my long-time friend, my rival . . . my *enemy*, Derek Klaus Hsu, as he raised his hands in triumph on his way to his third straight USA men's singles title. I'd forced a smile, shook his hand and his coach's, sat down, and

The Spirit of Pong

died. That's the only way to describe the feeling inside when all your training has ended in another defeat.

That's when I decided to go to China. I would have my whale.

I was the hardest worker the Maryland Table Tennis Center had ever seen. Training eight hours a day with some of the best coaches in America, seven days a week—I never took days off—plus physical training, sessions with sports psychologists, studying videos—these were supposed to make me the best. And I'd been the best. I remember beating Derek Klaus Hsu—for some reason everyone called him by all three names—at the USA Nationals in the under fourteen boys' singles final, winning deuce in the fifth on an edge ball. I'd raised my hands in triumph as he forced a smile, shook my hand and my coach's, sat down, and died. Little did we know that was the last time I'd ever beat him. Twelve years ago.

I was just a mid-level American player, the type that wows basement players and gets creamed by Chinese ball boys. I didn't have what it takes—in fact, as I know now, I didn't even know what it takes. I wouldn't know until Coach Wang taught me, or at least sent me to those who did. Yes, *that* Coach Wang. He was my coach.

The Chinese were the best. If I wanted to learn the secrets of table tennis, I had to go to China. To be specific, to the new National Table Tennis Training Center in Beijing, where the Chinese National Team trained. Somewhere in that building were the secrets I craved, secrets I needed, secrets I would *get*.

And so, on a cold day in January, I flew to Beijing, arriving as the sun went down. I used the last of my money for a taxi to the Training Center, thirty minutes away. And there it was!

It was beautiful—the Taj Mahal looked no better. China had had a national training center for decades, but the new one had only recently opened. I stared at it as I approached on the long walkway from the street.

Lights out front lit up a palace with pure white walls, perhaps two hundred feet wide, ten stories high, topped by a great white dome, with spires on all four corners. Towering bushes surrounded it. The bush by the door was cut into the

The Spirit of Pong

shape of a giant green ping-pong paddle and ball. On the right was a huge Chinese redwood tree that reached all the way to the top of the building and above. I could see the light coming out of the tenth floor, and could only wonder what was inside. For it was on the tenth floor that the national men's team trained. The women trained on the ninth, junior boys on the eighth, junior girls on the seventh, and various offices took up the first six. It was symbolic, having the players train on the upper floors, showing they were most important and above all others. Or so I'd read.

    I stood outside the front door, twiddling with my ping-pong paddle in the cold air. I stared at the ping-pong paddle bush and wondered what to do next. I had not told them I was coming, so they were not expecting me. Why would they want to train a mid-level American player in this Olympic sport? My job was to convince them. My stomach rumbled from nervousness and hunger. I had a packet of beef jerky in my pocket, and so pulled out a large hunk to chew on while I pondered my next move.

    Finally I took a deep breath and held my ear to the door—and I swear I could hear it! The distant sound of ping-pong balls getting hit back and forth. The balls were hitting rackets held by players coached by people who knew the secrets of table tennis. There was only one way to get those secrets.

    I knocked on the door.

    After a while I knocked again, and then I pounded on it. And then I waited.

    And waited.

    And waited.

    It was cold, and I was shivering, dressed in street clothes, with only a light warm-up jacket over the turtleneck shirt I always wore to hide the weird birthmark on my neck.

    I stared at the huge wooden door, wondering what to do next.

    "I believe I can help you," said a voice from behind me.

    I whirled around and there he was.

Chapter 2
The Sweat of Champions

He looked about my age. Like me, he held a paddle in his hand, but where I was twiddling with it, he was absentmindedly twirling it about like a baton in an absentminded fashion. He had that inscrutable Chinese look that screamed knowledge. A cigarette stuck out the corner of his mouth. He wore the red Dubai warm-up suit of the Chinese National Team, and yet I didn't recognize him. Hard to believe! He was still a nobody at that time.

"You are the American, Andy Blue?" he asked.

"You know me?" I asked. "They've heard of me in China?"

He shook his head. "Only I know of you. I know everything. I am Coach Wang."

He stared into my eyes like a searchlight, as if he could see into my soul. I kept eye contact, but I could feel my stomach tighten under this close scrutiny. He seemed young to be a high-level coach, but he was Chinese, and that had to count for something.

"What can I do for you?" I asked.

"What can I do for *you* is proper question," said Coach Wang. "You wish to be champion?"

"With every atom of my body," I said.

"Then I will make you champion. Come with me." He turned and walked down the walkway away from the National Training Center I had traveled almost 9000 miles to train at.

What was I supposed to do? The doorway to the National Training Center, the doorway to my dreams, was locked to me. My destiny did not lead in that direction, at least

The Spirit of Pong

not at this time. But someone once said that when one door closes, another one opens. I stared at Coach Wang's retreating back as he crossed the street, and made the fateful decision. I grabbed my few small bags and rushed after him.

It was a short trip as he walked into a small, run-down building across the street. It was only one floor, perhaps the size of a McDonalds. It had a large front window, and as I approached I saw the ping-pong tables inside. Another table tennis center!

But this one was small. I went inside and looked about. There were four tables, all vacant, and a small lounge area, also vacant except for Coach Wang, who now sat in a worn-out lounge chair that was probably older than me. There were several metal folding chairs, so I chose one and sat down. The place was poorly lit, a serious problem in an Olympic sport where the ball travels at speeds the eye can barely track.

"Welcome to my dojo, the Hall of Pong," he said. It was spookily quiet, without the usual sound of ping-pong balls being hit about. Perhaps it was just a slow night.

"You said you'd train me?" I asked. "I don't have any money."

Coach Wang shook his head. "I no want your money. I will make you champion. That will be my payment." He tossed out his cigarette and lit up another.

I looked about. The place was dirty—trash on the floor, chipped yellow paint from the walls on the floor, even cobwebs in one corner. I got up and examined the closest table. It was dusty, and obviously hadn't been used in some time. The other tables were the same.

I'd traveled halfway around the world for this? Even by American standards this was a dump. And yet, there was something about Coach Wang, something mysterious. If I'd only known.

"Do you accept me as your coach?" Coach Wang asked.

I'd dreamed of training under Chinese Head Coach Kong Guoliang, side by side with the members of the Chinese National Team at the National Training Center. Instead I was in a tiny, run-down dojo run by an unknown I'd met outside. This would be a life-changing decision.

The Spirit of Pong

Far more than I knew at the time.

"I accept you as my coach," I said as I wiped some dust away from a table. "When do we start?"

"We start now," he said, and I realized he was already at the far side, racket and ball in hand. We began to hit, forehand to forehand, a standard warm-up. Like me, he used a shakehands grip. Soon we'd get into more advanced stuff, and I'd learn the secrets of Chinese table tennis. Poor lighting, dusty tables, dirty floors—none of this mattered now.

"Should I change into my playing shoes?" I asked as we continued to hit.

"No need," he said. It felt funny playing in the running shoes that I used as my walking shoes when I wasn't playing. The heels made me an inch taller, and since I was so used to the thinner heels of my table tennis shoes I felt like I towered over the table. But if the coach said "no need," then who was I to question the coach? I was still in my traveling clothes, with my playing clothes in my bags.

"You have good form," he said after a few minutes.

"Thank you," I said, beaming on the inside.

"As your coach, I now know your game," he said, a small smile on his face.

"That was fast," I said.

"Is that a scar on your neck?" he asked, pointing with his free hand as we continued to rally.

"Just a birthmark." I'd been born with it. But the turtleneck shirt I wore was old and wearing out, and the neck had fallen down, revealing the weird mark.

"It looks like the mark of a rope on someone who was either strangled or hanged."

I shook my head; it was nothing so dramatic. "It was neither. I've had it since I was born. When I was a kid I used to cover it with makeup so the other kids wouldn't see. Now I just wear turtlenecks."

Coach Wang nodded. "You have the mark."

"What do you mean, 'the mark'?"

"And yet you are no good," he continued, ignoring me.

A punch to the gut. But it was true. A coach who can tell the truth is better than one who lies and gives false praise.

The Spirit of Pong

"And yet there is still hope," he said as we continued to hit forehand to forehand, never missing, a steady staccato rhythm as the ball went back and forth, back and forth. If I'd been a dog, my ears would have shot up.

"There are three secrets to table tennis," Coach Wang said. I smacked a forehand, harder than before. He caught the ball cleanly out of the air, finally ending our rally. "First you must have the Body of Pong." Inwardly I groaned and grinned at the same time. It was time for some physical training! It was the hardest part of training, pushing yourself to the max, sweating as you strained your muscles to their limit. But I was ready for the challenge. I wanted to be a champion. There was nothing he could ask me to do that I wouldn't do.

"Tell me what to do," I said. "What are the other two secrets?"

For the first time he smiled. "You will see. Now we go outside." It was time for some running! Conveniently I had on my running shoes—Coach Wang had foreseen this.

I followed him outside, ready to impress him with my running skills. I might not be able to beat the best players, but nobody trained harder.

He walked across the street, back to the Chinese National Training Center. I could almost hear the balls bouncing back and forth inside. Coach Wang stopped and pointed at the redwood tree on the side.

"You must climb tree and look through window," he said, puffing on his cigarette. He glanced at his watch and nodded to himself. "Hurry, it is almost time."

Climbing a tree for physical training? That wasn't something I'd done in America. Frankly, it seemed too easy. And why would I look through the window? But mine was not to question why, mine was just to climb and see why.

I was a professional athlete, and I climbed the tree with ease. When I reached the top, adjacent to the tenth floor, I waved at Coach Wang. He just stared back. It was time to look through the window.

In contrast to the Hall of Pong, the room was brightly lit. There were a number of tables in the huge room, each barriered off in large courts. But I barely noticed it because of who was

The Spirit of Pong

gathered around one of the tables, playing cards. It took me only seconds to see and recognize the greatest players in the world! But something was wrong, very wrong.

There was Bai Hanhui, the world champion, the best in the world, the most athletic of the Chinese, known for his incredible foot speed and powerful forehand. But there was something wrong, something different. Then it hit me—the man was overweight. Not overly fat, but nothing like the fit and thin Bai Hanhui I'd seen so many times.

Playing cards with him were three other legends. Fang Guiying, world #2, known for his powerful topspin from both forehand and backhand. Ping Qiao, world #3, known for his incredible quickness. And Yan Zhiheng, world #4, known for his incredible serves.

All seemed out of shape, nothing like the chiseled bodies of professional athletes. These were slightly bloated versions of the famous faces I'd worshipped from afar for so long. Yan in particular looked more Santa Claus than athlete.

And then in through a back door came Kong Guoliang, head coach of the Chinese Team, the legend himself, followed by three assistant coaches. Kong blew a whistle, and all four players jumped to their feet. Others that had been out of sight from my vantage point appeared, and soon the 24 members of the Chinese National Men's Team stood surrounding Coach Kong and the other coaches. One of the assistant coaches carried a case of water, which he placed on one of the tables—24 bottles of water, 24 members of the Chinese National Team, many of them obviously out of shape. Each grabbed a bottle and chugged it down.

And then, the impossible. Before my already disbelieving eyes came an even more disbelieving sight. The fat melted away like snow, leaving nothing behind but the chiseled bodies of the Chinese National Team as we all know them.

I glanced down at Coach Wang, who stood at the base of the redwood tree, and he smiled back. Then he motioned for me to climb down. I did so.

"What happened up there?" I asked as I reached the bottom and dropped to the ground.

The Spirit of Pong

"You have done physical training for many years," he said. "So have the Europeans and others all over the world. You have wasted your time. Now you know the truth. If you wish to be a champion, you need the Body of Pong. And there is only one way to do that."

"How?" I practically gasped.

"You must steal the training water," he said.

"You mean the case of water they were drinking?"

"Yes. But it is not water. It is the Sweat of Champions, collected during training, and fed to the players before training."

"Wait a minute. To get the Body of Pong, you want me to steal a case of water made of human sweat, and then *drink it?*" I felt sick to my stomach.

"There is more to it than that—you will see. But it is the only way. And take your playing bag with you, with racket and playing shoes."

"Why?"

"You will see." He had an irritating habit of answering many of my questions with those three mysterious words.

And so I had no choice. Coach Wang's plan was simple: I climb the tree late at night, break the window and climb in, and look around until I found a case of "training water," and steal it. Simple, right? But why did he insist on my bringing my playing bag? What was it I "will see"?

And so at midnight I found myself once again up at the top of the redwood tree, once again looking through the window, with my playing bag slung over my shoulder. The lights were off so I couldn't see inside. Coach Wang had given me a heavy flashlight which would serve two purposes. I stared at the window. Would this be the first step toward a life of crime? Breaking and entering was wrong, whether in America or China, and here I was, just a few hours after arriving. . . .

But it had to be done. I shinnied along a branch to the window. I took a long, smooth backswing with the heavy flashlight, almost like a forehand, and then put all my weight into smashing it into the window. It shattered into pieces. Then I hung back to see if anyone had heard. After about five minutes I decided it was safe. And that's how I finally got into the Chinese National Training Center, like a common burglar.

The Spirit of Pong

The gym was magnificent! There were twelve tables, two rows of six, all in full-sized playing courts, about fourteen by seven meters, each surrounded by waist-high barriers. This was where the best of the best trained, under the tutelage of the most brilliant coaches in the world. These were the playing courts of God.

I stared at them, feeling left out. But fate had intervened, and training here wasn't an option. I was now a disciple of Coach Wang, and a prospective thief. I was going to steal from the Gods.

No! I had to stop thinking of them as Gods. They were mere mortal men with great skills. Someday I was going to beat them. And if that meant stealing, so be it.

With flashlight in hand, I tiptoed through the courts where these Gods—mortal men—trained. A few rackets, towels, empty water bottles, and large numbers of balls lay scattered about.

With the flashlight I was able to see my way to the back door that Coach Kong and the other coaches had come through. There was a dimly lighted hallway on the other side. Coach Wang had told me to turn left and find the first door on the right.

This opened into a small, unlit office. With the flashlight I saw pictures of Coach Kong on the wall in his younger days, back when he dominated the world as one of the greatest players of all time. This was his office. Feeling braver now that I was five minutes or so into my criminal enterprise, I began to look about. I quickly went through the office, hoping to find the case of training water. In the back was a refrigerator. I opened it—and there they were! Three cases of water. The Sweat of Champions.

And then something growled, and I jumped three feet into the air.

Very slowly I pointed the flashlight in the direction of the sound, and saw the two very large dogs lying on the floor in a corner, their almond-shaped eyes reflecting the light of my flashlight like four bright coals. It was Ping and Pong, Coach Kong's pet Kunming wolfdogs, and the mascots of the Chinese

The Spirit of Pong

National Team. Slowly they rose to their feet, growling. They looked like German Shepherds but taller . . . and meaner.

"Nice doggies!" I said, wishing I knew how to say it in Chinese. The two wolfdogs growled louder, and took a few steps toward me, cornering me against the refrigerator. Their lips were curled back, exposing dozens of slobbering white teeth.

Very slowly I put down the flashlight and reached for a case of water. With my fingernails I tore a small hole in the plastic covering, which I slowly ripped wider. Then I reached in and grabbed a bottle. If I were going to have to fight a pair of wolfdogs, I'd need to be a lot faster than a normal human; I'd need the Body of Pong. And that meant drinking the Sweat of Champions—*and really fast!*

One of the wolfdogs lunged at me. With my normal table tennis reflexes I was able to push it aside, but the other followed. I smacked the second one in the head with the water bottle. Both began barking. Before they could come at me for round two, I twisted the lid off the bottle. The smell of sweat was instantly overpowering. The Chinese National Team Members *drank this?* I had no choice. I guzzled a large swallow. I began to heave, and probably would have thrown up if I hadn't been interrupted by round two as both dogs leaped at me, mouths wide.

The two dogs froze in mid-air, in mid-leap, slobbering jaws wide. Their howling was replaced by eerie silence. And then the silence was broken.

"You wish to train?" The voice, in only slightly accented English, came from the doorway. The silhouetted figure of a short man stood there. I stared back and forth between the two frozen dogs and the man in the doorway.

"Who are you?" I asked. I started to move my flashlight toward him.

He flipped on the light switch by the door. I could only stare in shocked recognition at the ghostly figure before me. He was relatively short and pencil thin, with thick eyebrows and a piercing stare. He wore a faded violet shirt.

No one from the table tennis world would have failed to recognize him, one of the most famous faces ever. The man who revolutionized table tennis in the 1950s with his training

The Spirit of Pong

methods and techniques, and who was so far ahead of his time that many are still used today. Who led Japan to years of dominance while twice winning Men's Singles at the World Championships. Whose training techniques were copied by the Chinese, who he also helped train, leading to their years of dominance. Who spent years as an executive member and then president of the International Table Tennis Federation, helping lead the sport from near obscurity to an Olympic Sport and greatness. And who had died in 1994. Every serious player remembers where he was when he first heard the great Ogi had died.

"You wish to train?" repeated the man. I could vaguely see the hallway behind his translucent figure. I'd recently read his biography, *Ogi: The Life of Ichiro Ogimura*. I felt like I was seeing a ghost, and I was.

And yet, this was the moment I'd been waiting for all my life. I was grateful for Coach Wang's help, but this was Ogimura. "*Yes!*" I cried.

"Come with me." He turned and walked into the hallway.

The Spirit of Pong

Chapter 3
Ogi

I followed him back to the training hall, my playing bag still slung over my shoulder. As we entered he flipped on the lights. I'd seen the hall earlier with my flashlight, but that didn't compare to what it looked like with the full lights blazing down on it. With such lighting you not only could follow a small, speeding ball, but even see the ball's spin.

The twelve tables were bright blue with blue nets. The gym had the red rubberized flooring designed for table tennis, with some padding so as not to hurt the knees, and very grippy for fast movement. The first five feet of the walls all the way around were light green, to give a good background for picking up the ball, and white above. On the wall was a giant picture of the Chinese flag—red with a big yellow star on the top left, with four smaller stars to the right—and the Olympics rings—blue, yellow, black, green, and red. The air had the gym smell I so loved.

Ogimura rummaged through a large playing bag and pulled out two things. The first was his own playing racket, a penhold blade. The second was a small framed painting. I watched as he stuck a pin in the wall under the Chinese flag picture and hung the picture. He did so somewhat awkwardly as his left non-playing arm couldn't seem to straighten out all the way—I vaguely remember reading about a childhood injury of his that caused that.

The Spirit of Pong

"Van Gogh," he said simply. Even I recognized *The Starry Night*, the famed painting of swirling stars.

Soon Ogimura and I faced each other across a table in the back corner. He appeared to be in his early twenties, at the peak of his career, but his eyes looked far older.

"You have drunk the Sweat of Champions," Ogimura said. "Now you must earn it. Now we train."

"You speak very good English," I said as I changed into my blue playing shoes—yes, I, Andy "Shoes" Blue, wore blue playing shoes. I knew that Ogimura had learned English early in life, and had even run a training camp in the U.S. in Grand Rapids, Michigan, in 1968, where he'd trained such U.S. stars as Dell and Connie Sweeris, D-J Lee, and John Tannehill. "Are you in fact Ogimura, or the ghost of Ogimura?"

"I am the spirit of Ogimura. You may call me Ogi."

"What's a Japanese spirit doing in a Chinese training center?" I asked.

"China is the center of table tennis."

We started off easy, hitting forehand drive to forehand drive, corner to corner. Nothing special there, just an easy warmup, as I'd done with Coach Wang.

"Now you loop," he said. A drive only has light topspin. Now I began grazing the ball more to create heavy topspin, a loop drive, one of the most advanced and most physical shots in table tennis. The topspin made the ball arc through the air, dropping on the other side like a rock and then jumping out with a quick, low bounce. Ogimura blocked them back with ease. This was somewhat surprising as the looping game hadn't been well developed during his playing days, but obviously he'd learned. At first I looped easy as I warmed up.

"Faster," he said. No problem; I would show him what I could do. I began to rotate my whole body into each shot, powering the ball with great speed and spin. In America, players struggled to block back more than a few of these; Ogimura continued to block them effortlessly. Then he began to block faster, so that his shots came out to me almost before I recovered from the previous shot.

The Spirit of Pong

"Faster!" he cried, and once again he picked up the pace. I could barely keep up with him, and I began to make mistakes. Each time I missed Ogimura would smile, and we'd start again.

"Now side to side," he declared, and began blocking one to my wide forehand, one to the middle of the table, a basic one-one forehand footwork drill, which I'd been doing daily most of my life. But his blocks were much quicker than I was used to, and once again I struggled to keep up, often having to lunge to get to each shot with my forehand.

"Faster!" he cried again. It was a mantra I would have to get used to. He increased the pace still more, so that his blocks were nearly smashes. They went wider and wider, forcing me to cover more and more table. I put everything I could into keeping up, but the pace was just too fast. Over and over he caught me out of position, and the rally would end as his block ended up at the wall behind me. Soon I was breathing heavily, and the rallies were ending far too soon. Finally, in mid-rally, after I barely made a lunging return, he caught the ball.

"You are slow and out of shape," he declared, shaking his head. "You are too old. Yes. Perhaps you are too old to begin the training?"

I felt my face grow red. "I'm not lazy and I'm not too old! Nobody trains harder than me."

"And yet you are a slow, out-of-shape American."

How could the great Ogimura say this to me? "I'm not out of shape!'

"Then do one hundred laps. Around the gym. *Now!*"

I slammed my racket down on the table and began to jog.

"Faster!"

Okay, I'd show him. I took off at a sprint. I knew I couldn't keep up that pace for one hundred laps, but I'd push myself to the limit.

"Faster!" he cried as I finished the tenth lap.

"I'm running as fast as I can!"

"Says the slow, out-of-shape American." He pointed his finger at me and spoke very slowly, his words reverberating like an echo over the gym. "*You must dig in deep.*"

The Spirit of Pong

I realized I'd slowed to a jog. I took one deep breath, and took with everything I had. I kept this up for twenty laps, then I began to labor.

"*Faster! You can do this!*"

Somehow I found a reserve of energy, and I took off again. But after sprinting five more laps I was done. I collapsed to the floor.

"You have completed thirty-five laps," Ogimura said in a mild voice. "You waste my time." Then he raised his voice. "*Get up!*"

Slowly I rose to my feet, still breathing heavily, my legs already dead. Ogimura's dark eyes bore into me.

"You have drunk the Sweat of Champions," he said. "You have reserves you know nothing about. *Continue!*"

Somehow I began to run again. Sixty-five laps to go. I completed another lap, but not quite at full speed. Then, as Ogimura opened his mouth, I put whatever I had left into it, and took off in a sprint.

In a storybook, I would have sprinted the last sixty-four laps. The reality is that after all-out sprinting four more laps, I collapsed again, and this time I mean really collapsed, gasping in exhaustion.

Ogimura was shaking his head, and yet he was smiling. "Good, good."

"What was good?" I asked, gulping in air.

"You nearly killed yourself trying," he said.

"I always do that," I said.

"I know," he said. "But if you want to be champion, *you must be willing to die for it*. And now we begin again."

"What do you mean?"

"You have sixty more laps to go. And then we begin the real training."

Somehow I got through those sixty laps, helped by Ogimura's cries of "*Faster!*" anytime I let up. I collapsed again after eighty laps, but was up within thirty seconds, and then managed to finish the laps—sprinting the last lap at a speed I wouldn't have believed possible. Then I collapsed to the floor. It had been the hardest training session of my life.

"Now we train," Ogimura said.

The Spirit of Pong

"What?"

"*On your feet!*" And so it was back to the table, with more drills.

"What's needed isn't extraordinary ability," he said, "but extraordinary effort. Can you give me that?"

"*Yes!*" I said, feeling like a marine recruit. And so the real training began.

Every drill involved moving, and always faster than I had ever moved before. He not only wanted my shots to have more speed but more topspin as well, which meant putting more and more power into each shot to get the necessary speed and spin. The only breaks were occasional water fountain and bathroom breaks. The drills were relentless, and the pace faster and faster. My wobbly legs couldn't keep up, but somehow I kept at it. I lost track of time, but it must have been the early morning hours when he finally caught the ball.

"Wait here." He left the gym for a few minutes, then returned with two plates of rice, with bits of chicken and vegetables mixed in. He handed me one of plates and a pair of chopsticks.

I stabbed at the rice with a chopstick, but it was like poking at smoke with an umbrella. Holding a chopstick in each hand, I managed to lift a chunk of rice with a piece of chicken. But as I raised it to my mouth the food fell off and onto the floor. This was archaic, trying to eat with a pair of sticks.

"Coach Ogi, do you have a fork?" I asked.

"If you cannot learn to eat with chopsticks, you cannot learn table tennis."

I watched as he rapidly shoveled the rice into his mouth, far faster than I could with a fork. At one point he slowed down, and gave me a glimpse of how he held them. I copied it as best I could, but it was like trying to thread a needle while wearing ski gloves. I fumbled through the meal as an amused Ogimura watched. He had another unfair advantage in that he played table tennis with the penhold grip, which uses the same hand and finger muscles as when using chopsticks.

"Now you sleep." He pointed at the table we'd been training on.

The Spirit of Pong

"You want me to sleep under the table?" I asked. "Won't the Chinese team be coming in soon to train?"

"Don't worry about them."

"Shouldn't I let Coach Wang know I'll be staying here?"

Ogimura smiled. "Yes, it would be Coach Wang. Don't worry about him. He knows."

"He knows what?"

"He knows that you'll be staying here for a year."

It took a few seconds for that to sink in. "*A year?*"

"Do you wish to be champion?"

That was a no-brainer. "*Yes!*"

"Then I will train you for one year. And then, maybe, just maybe, if you don't quit and I don't throw you out in disgust, you will have the Body of Pong."

The Spirit of Pong

Chapter 4
The Body of Pong

And so the year of training began. Each night I'd sleep under the table, on the hard floor with nothing but a pillow and blanket that Ogimura gave me. Strangely neither the Chinese team nor anyone else ever entered the gym—it was just the two of us, day after day, seven days a week, for 52 straight weeks. Each morning Ogimura would arrive right at sun-up, with another rice meal for breakfast, with chicken, beef, pork, or fish mixed in. I'd be up and showered before he arrived, with fresh clothes he'd brought me. Then we'd train until lunchtime. Then he'd leave for a few minutes, and he'd return with a rice meal for lunch. Then we'd train until dinner. Then he'd leave again, and return with still another rice meal for dinner. After dinner we'd train another three hours. Afterwards he'd always mop up the floor, which was covered in my sweat, and then he'd leave, and I'd collapse under the table and fall asleep in seconds.

I learned to hate rice.

But a strange thing happened. After a few weeks of this I found myself shoveling the rice into my mouth nearly as fast as Ogimura. At first he seemed amused by this. But then I began eating faster than him—and he responded by increasing his speed, leaving me in the dust. And then every meal became a race. Each time I thought I'd caught up to him he'd increase his speed, and always he'd finish his meal first.

Often at night I'd have dreams of ping-pong. Always they involved training, often harder than the real training where I was limited by my physical body. Often the dreams ended with me on a boat, out at sea, the salty smell of sweat replaced by the salty sea air, searching, always searching, for the whale.

One night I thought I sighted the whale, and raised my harpoon—a puny ping-pong paddle—but something woke me up; the familiar sound of balls bouncing off tables and rackets, including my own table. I crawled out from under it, and there

The Spirit of Pong

they were, 24 ghostly figures, two on each table. I recognized all of these Chinese greats from the past.

> Zhuang Zedong and Li Furong.
> Rong Guotuan and Xu Yinsheng.
> Xi Enting and Liang Geliang.
> Li Zhenshi and Chen Xinhua.
> Guo Yuehua and Cai Zhenhua.
> Jiang Jialiang and Chen Longcan.
> Teng Yi and Wang Tao.
> Kong Linghui and Liu Guoliang.
> Wang Liqin and Ma Lin.
> Wang Hao and Liu Guozheng.
> Fan Zhendong and Xu Xin.
> Zhang Jike and Ma Long.

Most of these champions were still alive, so who, or what, was playing on the tables? I would later learn. For now I just watched these great champions as they rallied. At first they were training hard, taking turns doing footwork drills and then serve and receive drills. But toward the end they began to have fun, and took turns lobbing and smashing. At one point Kong Linghui lobbed balls back over and over while sitting in the very window I'd broken to get in, while Liu Guoliang smashed over and over, before ending the rally with a backspin drop shot that came back into the net as Kong applauded from the windowsill. After watching them for a while I went back to bed. It seemed only natural that these other spirits would want to get their own playing time in.

The training only grew in intensity. "You mustn't dilly-dally," he'd say if he didn't think I was training at full intensity. I wondered where he'd picked up that term. "*Faster!*" he'd cry every few minutes. Like most top players, my forehand was more powerful than my backhand, and so he trained me to cover as much of the table with it as possible, which meant non-stop footwork drills as he relentlessly moved me side to side, faster and faster, and I was expected to move to each ball and throw myself into each shot, unleashing one powerful forehand loop

The Spirit of Pong

drive after another. But he also trained my backhand, forcing me to attack and counter-attack with it as well. He also worked on my defense, forcing me to return his hardest smashes, often with my own counter-smashes or loop drives.

He'd admonish me if I made too many mistakes. "Do not make the same mistake twice. Even worms never go back to the same place once they've had an electric shock."

Besides the relentless training at the table we also did physical training. Every day I'd do the hundred laps, and later two hundred. Then came various jumping exercises that at first seemed insane as I'd frog jump around the gym over and over, later on with weights on my back. Then he'd bring out a jump rope and have me do double and eventually triple jumps at speeds I never would have believed possible. There were weights in a corner, and so every day I did weight training.

We also did lots of shadow practice, where I'd practice my shots away from the table, with no ball, just me and the racket. He'd have me play simulated matches at breakneck speeds, with him calling out the shots as I tried to perform to his standards. He also introduced me to the infamous "seven strokes in five seconds" drill, something I'd heard of but which had never really registered. There were a number of variations, but all involved the obvious—seven very fast strokes in five seconds, performed over and over for up to two hours straight. Not short, quick strokes, but full-body acrobatic ones. The only breaks were our rice-eating race meals, eight hours sleep, and serve practice.

Every day I looked forward to serve practice. It was the only training that didn't involve digging in deeper and deeper, to levels of unimaginable pain. Twice a day we'd practice serves for half an hour. But now his cries were *"More spin!"* Through years of practice I'd developed spinny serves, but nothing satisfied him; he wanted more. I could serve with topspin, backspin, sidespin, and various combinations, all done with a very fast motion so the opponent couldn't easily see what type of spin I was doing.

"Did you know that a ping-pong ball spins faster than an airplane propeller?" he asked. I didn't. After about a month of this, he seemed to be happier with the spin on my serves—and

The Spirit of Pong

then he went back to his old cry of "*Faster!*" And so my serving motion became faster and faster, making it harder for an opponent to pick up on the contact and type of spin.

He also worked on my fast, deep serves, stressing speed and accuracy. He'd put a broken ball on the far corner of the table, and he'd challenge me to knock it off with a fast serve, one hundred times in a row. If I missed, the count started over at zero. When I finally did one hundred in a row, he clapped and cheered like I'd just won the World Championships. Then he brought out a cloth, tied it over my eyes, and challenged me to do it again. I thought he was crazy, but after months of training, I knocked the ball off the table blindfolded fifty-two times in a row.

"Here in China," he said, "they don't call the first shot of a rally the 'service'—they call it the 'launch.' They think of the serve as the first chance to launch an attack. We in Japan were too soft in adopting the English word 'service' for the first shot."

When I wasn't sleeping, eating rice meals, or practicing serves, it was always hard training, either footwork training at the table, or physical training away.

"Set a personal best each day," he said. Sure enough, at the end of each day he'd ask me what personal bests I'd set, and I learned I'd better have one.

"If you wish to be a champion, you must eat, drink, and breathe table tennis," he'd say. It was all we talked about; it was all we thought about. He was a hard trainer, but he was also encouraging, telling me I could do the impossible, and it always became possible. He was like Mr. Miyagi from *The Karate Kid*.

"The body and mind are one," he said. "You must train your body so that your mind can use it as a weapon. Later you will learn how to train your mind." A wistful expression came over him. "I actually enjoy teaching that part more, but it's not my turn."

"What do you mean, Coach Ogi?"

"Never mind." Then he went into a lecture on the need to focus during training, something he'd harp on the rest of our time together.

The Spirit of Pong

He was also a master of multiball training. He'd stand to the side of the table, with a box of balls on the table. Then he'd grab the balls in rapid succession and hit them to my side of the table in various patterns. This allowed him to hit the balls even faster than would be possible in a real rally—and he was relentless with this, hitting balls far beyond what I'd see in a real game, and expecting me to react to balls that were humanly impossible to react to. And yet, after a time, and numerous cries of "*Faster!*", I begin to react more quickly and even make strong returns. I was digging in deep, and finding those reserves that Ogimura had said were there. If he wanted extraordinary effort, that's what he'd get.

One time, after our night training, Ogimura didn't leave. Instead he pulled a record player from his bag and an actual record—a large, flat disk with grooves. I'd seen one once, in my grandfather's attic, and he'd told me what it was, but I'd never seen one actually played. Ogimura put on *Nobody Knows the Trouble I've Seen* by Louis Armstrong. We sat down and listened to it and other Armstrong recordings for a bit; Ogimura turned out to be quite a fan. He'd also brought rice balls wrapped in seaweed, a Chinese delicacy, and Old Parr Scotch Whiskey. We listened and ate and drank. I wasn't much of a drinker, and only sipped the whisky, but Ogimura took big swags of it.

"Artists express the universe through brushstrokes, violinists through sound," he said, slightly slurring his words. "We express the universe through table tennis . . . We don't play table tennis just to win. We swing our rackets to elevate human culture." And then, perhaps a bit drunk, he turned the record player off, rose to his feet, and stunned me by expertly singing the English ballad *Danny Boy*.

"Now it's your turn," he said when he'd finished.

"Sorry, I'm not a singer. I only play table tennis."

"Yesterday, today, and tomorrow, you are a table tennis player. But tonight you are a singer."

"Not a chance!"

Ogimura gave me his piercing stare. "If you don't have the guts to sing in front of another person, you'll never win a match."

The Spirit of Pong

I didn't see the connection, but he was serious. "What should I sing?"

"Anything, as long as you do it with full effort."

I thought for a moment. I really didn't have many options. Finally, I sang about the only song I knew the lyrics to. And so began my first semi-public rendition of *Mary Had a Little Lamb*. I didn't just sing it; I belted it out at full throttle, putting every ounce of energy I could into it. When I finished the four stanzas, four lines each, I gave a little bow and sat down.

"Wonderful!" Ogimura cried. From there on, once a week, we had our little parties, just Ogimura, me, Danny Boy, Mary and her lamb, rice balls, and whiskey.

Each day I put a mark on the wall, counting off the days. Since the sponge covering on my racket wore out from all the training, every two weeks he supplied me with two new sheets to glue on to replace the old sheets. My table tennis shoes wore just as fast, and soon he was bringing me a new pair every two weeks as well. And finally, after 52 sheets of sponge, 26 pairs of shoes, and unknown quantities of sweat, I put mark number 365 on the wall, and began our final day of training.

As usual Ogimura brought in our rice meals, this time with chicken, my favorite. Once again we raced. We battled to the very end, like two rice transporting machines. When he put the final clump of rice in his mouth, I was only a second behind. He smiled in victory and gave me a pat on the shoulder. Not bad for an American with one year training against one of the most competitive people in the history of sports. A personal best for the day, but there'd be more.

As I'd done for months now, I sprinted the two hundred laps. I frog jumped as only a super-frog could. I lifted more weights than I'd ever believed possible. I did a thousand consecutive triple jumps on the jump rope. I knocked the ball off the table with my fast serve one hundred times in a row on the first try. And no matter how fast Ogimura hit his shots, I was always there. He never once said *"Faster!"*

Ogimura bowed to me. "You now have the Body of Pong. You have taken the first step."

The Spirit of Pong

I started to bow back, and then his words hit me. "The *first* step?"

He smiled. "You have a long way to go. The way will not be easy. But I have something that will help." He gestured to a corner, where three cases of bottled water were stacked. "That is your sweat. It is now the Sweat of Champions. Sip it before your matches, and you will always have the Body of Pong. It will always be there for you, as will I."

"Does everyone on the Chinese team have the Sweat of Champions?"

"Of course," he said. "But they have grown fat and lazy, relying on their past sweat for their performance. They ate too many mooncakes during the Harvest Festival. This puts them at a disadvantage against one who starts in great shape *and* has the Sweat of Champions."

He walked over to the wall, under the Chinese flag picture, to where he'd hung the Van Gogh painting so long ago. He stared at it for a moment, and then took it down. Then he turned to me, *The Starry Night* in one hand, his paddle in the other, and faded out. I was left alone.

Or was I? I heard footsteps, and the door to the gym opening. I grabbed my playing bag and the three cases of sweat, and made for the window. Someone yelled at me in Chinese, and I looked back. It was Coach Kong Guoliang! It had been a year since I'd seen anyone other than Ogimura. At his side were the two Kunming wolfdogs, Ping and Pong, who charged, howling like angry banshees who'd been cheated out of a meal—me, one year ago.

The window was still broken from a year before when I'd broken in. With my new Body of Pong I had no trouble climbing through the window despite the three heavy cases of water. Kong followed, but I leaped to the redwood tree, climbed through its branches to the trunk, and began shinnying down, even as he yelled at me in Chinese. Soon I reached the ground. I ran across the street to the Hall of Pong. The sun was just rising, which made no sense since I had just finished my after-dinner session with Ogimura, and it should have been around 10PM.

Coach Wang was waiting for me, a cigarette in his mouth and a big smile on his face. "Did you have a good night?"

The Spirit of Pong

Coach Wang had meant that literally; I had spent one night at the Chinese National Training Center, and yet in that one night I had trained for a year with Ogimura. He took me to a breakfast diner down the street, and for the first time in a year—or a day—I ate something other than a rice meal. I dug into a plate of scrambled eggs and waffles like a man possessed, and possessed I might have been, having trained with a ghost for a year.

Coach Wang was in a very good mood. I began to tell him about my training with Ogimura, but he hushed me. "I learned from my coach, who learned from his coach, who learned from his coach. But in the beginning, we all learned from Ogimura."

But then the smile was gone from Coach Wang's face. "You now have the Body of Pong. Now you must learn the second secret of Chinese Table Tennis. You must have the Mind of Pong."

The Spirit of Pong

Chapter 5
The Mind of Pong

"We must go to Zhuhai City in Guangdong," Coach Wang said.

"What's in Guangdong?" I asked. "Is that were I'll get the Mind of Pong?"

"Yes."

This sounded like a combination of developing tactical thinking and sports psychology. I'd already read the classic book on tactics, *Table Tennis Tactics for Thinkers*, and all the major sport psychology books. Whatever Coach Wang had in mind for me, I was ready.

I assumed we'd jump in a car and drive to wherever we were going. Which shows how well I know Chinese geography. I knew that Beijing was toward the north in China, and like a typical American, assumed anywhere worth going to in a foreign country was within driving distance.

Zhuhai City was on the very bottom of China, on the coast of the South China Sea—over 1200 miles away. And so we were off to the airport. I never even had a chance to unpack. Heck, I'd never arranged a place to stay in China, assuming that after the Chinese saw my potential and how hard I worked, they'd find me a place to stay. I wasn't thinking too clearly—high aspirations have a tendency to do that.

32

The Spirit of Pong

"I think I told you I don't have any money," I said.

"Is no problem," Coach Wang said. "I pay."

Coach Wang was wonderful in so many ways. He paid for the taxi to the airport, for the airline tickets, and for meals. I'd never felt so appreciated. All this for me!

But whenever I asked what we'd be doing in Zhuhai City, I'd get the usual "You will see," or he'd just ignore me in his Chinese inscrutable way. If I kept bugging him about it, I'd sound like a loud-mouth American, so I finally stopped, and spent most of the trip dreaming about future glory before dozing off.

When we arrived that afternoon we had a great meal at a McDonalds—they're all over China—and then caught a taxi. We stopped at Zhuhai Sports Center Park, next to a large bronze statue of a man on a pedestal. He wore a suit, and carried a large trophy cup in his left arm, a bouquet of flowers in his right. I couldn't read the caption about the man.

"This is Rong Guotuan," said Coach Wang. "Do you know of him?"

Did I know of him? "Of course!" I cried. "The 1959 world men's singles champion, China's first. A penholder with great hitting and blocking. One of the great champions in our sport." I grew silent as I looked at the statue. I wondered if the great man was still alive.

"And?" asked Coach Wang.

"And what?"

He shook his head. "Is that all Americans know of Rong Guotuan?" He slammed a cigarette stub to the ground.

"I'm sorry. What should I know?"

Coach Wang lit another cigarette and then paced back and forth for a few minutes before breaking the silence. "He coached Chinese Women's Team to their first world team title at 1965 World Championships. He was great player, great tactician, great coach, and great patriot. Like Ogimura, Zhuang Zedong, and a few others, he was a Master of Pong."

"Where is he now?"

"You will learn." We returned to the taxi. This time we stopped at a graveyard. I realized I had my answer about whether Rong was alive.

The Spirit of Pong

We soon found his grave. Even in the Chinese I could make out the numbers and saw that he'd lived a short life: August 10, 1937 to June 20, 1968. He'd died at age 30, nine years after winning men's singles at the Worlds, three years after coaching the women's team to the world title.

"How did he die?" I asked.

Coach Wang looked angry. "In Cultural Revolution Rong was framed as spy. Condemned and tortured. He hanged himself. The same happened to Fu Qifang, coach of one of our greatest champions, Zhuang Zedong, and to Jiang Yongning, because they found a picture of him with a Japanese flag on his uniform—*from when he was a boy*. All were falsely accused, arrested, disgraced, tortured, and all three committed suicide in 1968. These things should *not* be forgotten!"

I stared at the grave marker, and then below it, where presumably the body of this greatly wronged man now lay. What a horrible thing. I began to shake in anger. Or did I? Then I realized it was not I that was shaking, but the ground.

I began to back away, but Coach Wang, who stood behind me, put a hand on my back. "Stay."

And so I stayed, and watched as a mist came out of the shaking ground. It rose up, and gradually took on the vague outlines of a man. I could barely make out the features, which resembled the statue and the many pictures I'd seen of Rong.

Then the mist flowed toward me like a gust of wind, and entered me directly through my forehead. I felt a shock, and took a step back. I felt electric shocks in my brain, and tiny explosions like fireflies in front of my eyes, like a mini Fourth of July fireworks display.

Then my head exploded as if the fireworks were inside. I fell to the ground, howling like the wolfdogs. It was agony that could not be described, only felt and perhaps imagined in a person's worst nightmare times a hundred.

And then I was in a classroom. One moment I'd been sitting at a Chinese graveyard, my head exploding in agony, and the next I was sitting in a chair before a small desk. Standing in front was a Chinese man in what I recognized as an old-style red Chinese warm-up suit. He was tall and skinny, like a scarecrow, with a long face with big eyes, and like Ogimura, slightly

The Spirit of Pong

translucent. Behind him was a blackboard. I looked around and saw that a ping-pong table was set up in the back of the classroom. I was the only student.

"Are you the spirit of Rong Guotuan?" I asked.

He bowed slightly.

"Am I going to be here for a year?" I was not looking forward to this.

Again he bowed slightly.

"Do you speak English?"

"I speak whatever language you speak, American. I have seen you many times, sleeping under the table during your time with Ogimura, while I practiced."

"I saw you once, hitting with Xu Yinsheng." After his playing career, Xu would spend decades as president of the Chinese Table Tennis Association, and like Ogimura, he would serve as president of the International Table Tennis Federation.

"Xu was a great champion and great leader. Now, American, do you choose to serve or receive?"

"What do you mean?"

"Do you choose to serve or receive? I cannot be clearer."

"Do you mean at the start of a match?"

"No, at the end of a match." He shook his head. "Another stupid American. Of course at the start of a match!"

A rocky start. But things hadn't gone so well at the start with Ogimura either.

"I always serve first. I like to get a lead."

"Why would you care if you got a lead as long as you were able to regain the lead when you serve? Or are you mentally weak and afraid to play from behind?"

"No! At least, I don't think so."

"When is a player most likely to make mistakes?"

I thought it over, wondering if it was a trick question. "Two times. At the very start of a match, when he's not yet fully warmed up or adjusted to his opponent. And at the end of a close game, when there's pressure."

Rong nodded. "Very good, American. So let us analyze this. You are most likely to make mistakes at the very start of a match. If you serve first, then you are likely to waste your serve,

35

The Spirit of Pong

and then your opponent, more warmed up and adjusted to you then you were to him, now gets to serve. And so you start at a disadvantage. Do this make sense to you, American?"

"Yes."

"Would you prefer to serve or receive at the end of a close game?"

"Serve."

"If you serve first, in close games you will be serving at the end of the second and fourth games of a best of five. If you receive first, you will be serving at the end of the first, third, and fifth games. Three times versus two. Is three greater than two, American?"

"Yes it is."

"Do you choose to serve or receive, American?"

"I choose to receive." For some reason I'd never really thought it through like this. I guess I was a stupid American. But I wasn't going to stay a stupid American. "But aren't there exceptions? Suppose the opponent is mentally weak, and plays better with a lead? Then I might want to serve first."

Rong nodded. "Good, American, there is hope for you."

And so it began. I already knew much of what he said in his slow, sometimes condescending way, and yet, just when I was nodding my head at some obvious statement he'd make, he'd go into aspects I'd never thought of. It was very quickly obvious that he wasn't stuck in tactics from his era; he was up to date with the modern game. Before, *Table Tennis Tactics for Thinkers* had always seemed like the final word on all things tactical, but now it seemed more like Dr. Seuss.

Speed was good; that he stressed over and over in agreement with Ogimura. But speed alone is predictable and a worthy opponent can adjust to any pace. Changing the pace made speed even more effective. And so we'd alternate between theoretical discussions, often with Rong using the blackboard to diagram rallies in chalk, and the table in the back, where we'd play them out. Always his blackboard theories worked out.

Spin was good; that he also stressed over and over in agreement with Ogimura. But spin alone is predictable and a worthy opponent can adjust to any spin. Changing the spin made spin even more effective, even using no-spin as a variation,

The Spirit of Pong

but disguising it as spin by using a big motion to fool the opponent. Once again we alternated between theoretical discussions in front of the blackboard, where he'd diagram the various spins we'd use, and then we'd play those spins on the table in back.

"Tactics is not just knowing, it is doing," he said. "You must train your subconscious to react tactically." And so we'd practice various scenarios, over and over, until I reacted with just the right tactic each time. It wasn't enough to make a strong loop; it had to be to the right place on the table, often with a fake the other way. Sometimes a strong loop wasn't what was called for; why go for a difficult fast loop when an opponent is ready for it, when a slower one would set up an easier winner?

"You must observe the habits of your opponent," he said. "When you played Derek Klaus Hsu in your last match, what did you notice about his serve? Take your time to answer."

I thought about it. Like most top players, he mostly served short, often to the middle, mostly with a forehand pendulum motion. But there was one thing that he did that really gave me trouble.

"About three times a game he served this fast, breaking serve to my backhand," I said. "His motion is almost the same as his short serve. It took me most of the match to get used to it, and even then my returns were too soft, and he'd rip them. I think I need to practice against someone with serves like those or I'll always have trouble with them."

Rong was nodding his head. "Good. You know you have to practice and to learn. But tactics is often the art of the simple. You saw his serve, but you did not see it. What did you *not* see?"

I thought hard, but couldn't think of anything. "I don't know."

"When he's about to serve fast and long, as he prepares for the extra effort, his tongue sticks out slightly from his mouth. Always. And that is why you lost—not because you did not see this simple thing, but because you are not in the *habit* of seeing simple things." And then he played video of my last match with Derek Klaus Hsu, somehow right there on the blackboard. And sure enough, there was his tongue sticking out slightly before every deep serve. I'd played matches before where

The Spirit of Pong

I'd noticed an opponent had a longer backswing when serving long and took advantage of it, but nothing like this.

It seemed like he'd seen every match I'd ever played, perhaps every match ever played by anyone. He could go on and on about each of them.

"Tactical thinking is a habit," he said after watching me lose a match where I attacked nearly everything. "You could have won that match if you'd blocked more."

"If I want to be the best," I said, "I have to play like the best, and they would have attacked those balls, even if it meant losing.

"If you want to be the best," Rong said, "you have to think like the best, and they would have played smart, and they would have won."

"Isn't that short-term thinking, trying to win now, instead of preparing for the future?"

"Learning to think tactically *is* preparing for the future. You have to develop both your physical *and* tactical game, and so you have to practice *both*."

It was an interesting way of looking at things. "But where do you find the balance?"

"That is the best question you have ever asked. Tactical thinking is about finding ways to win now. Strategic thinking is about developing weapons for later. But part of strategic thinking is developing the tactical skills for later." He pointed at me. "You are a good player who plays good tactics. If you want to be a *great* player, you must learn *great* tactics. It is not either-or, it is both. When you find that balance, *that* is when you will find greatness."

This was the closest thing to a compliment he'd ever given me. But he was right, I wasn't after goodness; I trained for greatness. And that meant great in all things, including the mental game.

Every day he'd have dozens of mantras, with examples to back them up. For example, he'd say, "Tactics is sifting through an incredible number of possible tactics and finding a few simple ones that work." And then we'd spend hours reviewing matches and finding such simple tactics. Sometimes

The Spirit of Pong

we'd watch a match I'd lost, and I could only say "D'oh!" as he pointed out the obvious simple things I'd missed.

But it wasn't just tactics. Mental training included preparing the mind for combat. "Always focus," he said, "for without focus, there is nothing." And then he'd rally with me while throwing balls at me with his free hand, trying to break my focus—successfully at first, but soon I learned to ignore them. If I appeared to lose my focus, he'd say, "*Nothing* in the universe matters except the next shot. Focus only on that." Concentration, he explained, was as much a part of the Mind of Pong as tactics.

I slept under the ping-pong table in the back, once again on the hard floor with a pillow and blanket that Rong gave me. Once again it was back to rice meals, to my great disgust. No chopstick races; Rong took his time when he ate, so I always finished first.

At first I found myself often arguing with Rong, but contrary to his name, he was seemingly never wrong. I tired of his often sarcastic responses, which always ended with a somehow derogatory "American." And so one morning I vowed to stop arguing, and to just listen and learn.

"Why aren't you arguing with me?" he asked that afternoon. When I explained I thought it best for me to just listen and learn, he shook his head in disgust. "Stupid American! How can you learn if you just sit back and accept everything! If you disagree, say you disagree. If you don't understand, say you don't understand. Otherwise you will always be a stupid American."

And so I went back to my argumentative ways.

"Find ways to use your best weapons," he said another time after watching another of my long-ago matches where I'd won by blocking—not by choice, but because my opponent had somehow kept me from attacking. I didn't even remember the opponent's name.

"But I won that match!" I exclaimed.

"But not by as much as you would have if you had played smart," he said. "You won, but you practiced playing stupid. What happens when you play someone with that style

The Spirit of Pong

who *is* good enough to beat you? That was practice time wasted."

"But the guy kept dropping my short backspin serves short, and kept me from attacking. When I tried short sidespin-topspin, he attacked it. So I served long, and blocked him down. It was smart tactical thinking."

"No, it was dumb tactical thinking, because it was based on a false premise," Rong said. "Why was he able to drop your serve short? Watch again."

And so we replayed the match—and it hit me. "My short serves are mostly all backspin."

He nodded. "And so he easily drops them short. If you mixed in short no-spin serves, he would have another option to worry about, and he wouldn't have had such good control. Plus you only served to the middle and backhand, almost never short to the forehand, making things even easier for him."

"But if I serve short to the forehand he has an angle into my forehand," I pointed out. "To guard against that I have to edge toward my forehand side. So all he has to do is return it down the line and he takes away my forehand. Your tactics takes away my best shot."

Again he nodded. "Good thinking. Which is why you only serve short to the forehand as a *variation*. That way he won't get used to it and so won't receive it well. Plus he'll have to watch for that serve, and so won't be as ready when he receives with his backhand. It is all about balance."

We had many arguments, and to this day there are a few small items where I think maybe, just maybe, I was right, and he was wrong.

But probably not.

"If you want to learn the art of table tennis, you must learn the art of war," he said one day. At first I thought he meant this metaphorically. But he handed me a book, *The Art of War* by Sun Tzu, a famous Chinese general from 2500 years ago. The first chapter was on *Detail Assessment and Planning*, and pretty much explained how to prepare for a match. It went on through *Waging War, Strategic Attack, Disposition of the Army, Forces, Weaknesses and Strengths, Military Maneuvers, Variations and Adaptability, Movement and Development of Troops, Terrain, The Nine*

The Spirit of Pong

Battlefields, Attacking with Fire, and ended with *Intelligence and Espionage*, which essentially told you how to go about scouting a table tennis opponent. The thirteen chapters were almost a manual for table tennis, once you translated into table tennis terms. For example, when it talks about armies and troops, in table tennis that means your shots—serves, forehands, backhands, and so on. When it talks about terrain, that meant the various places on the table—short, long, forehand side, backhand side, middle, and so on. Someday someone's going to actually translate this into table tennis language and sell a million copies.

Like before, I marked off the days. The days went by more quickly than with Ogimura. It wasn't that Rong was any easier on me mentally than Ogimura had been on me physically. I realized that the year with Ogimura had trained my mind as well as my body, and so the daily work with Rong didn't seem so difficult.

I would have my whale.

"How come you teach the Mind of Pong, and Ogimura the Body of Pong?" I asked one day. I'd heard that both were master tacticians and training fanatics.

"We take turns," Rong said. "Sometimes Ogimura teaches, sometimes me, sometimes Zhuang Zedong or others. Even European champions sometimes, like Stellan Bengtsson. And then there is the Dragon."

"Who is that?"

"Forget that, you must focus on your work *here!*" Rong cried. And from there on he regularly reminded me to focus if I so much as looked away.

And then the year was up. Rong erased the last bit of theoretical chalk marks off the blackboard, and nodded.

"Do I now have the Mind of Pong?" I asked.

"It is not that easy, American. First you must pay my price."

"Ogimura didn't charge me. And I don't have any money."

"Ogimura was a great man, and he lived a great life. I might have been a great man and lived a great life, but it was stolen from me."

The Spirit of Pong

I remembered what Coach Wang had said, and the bitterness he'd shown at the treatment Rong had received.

"You were a great man," I said. "But I am not to blame for what happened to you."

"No you are not, American. But if you wish to have the Mind of Pong, you will pay my price. Do you wish to be a champion?"

Once again that was a no-brainer. "*Yes!*"

"Then pay the price, American."

Chapter 6
The Red Guards

Suddenly I was on a raised platform next to a street. Hundreds of people surrounded me, pelting me with rocks. "Traitor!" they cried. The rocks hit, but for some reason I couldn't move. More insults and accusations were thrown at me—I was a spy and a disgrace to the Revolution. The rocks and words continued to fly.

They were only words, but they were more than words. The rocks hurt with terrible pain, but the words were agonizing. I was a patriot. I'd represented my country, China, with honor, winning world titles and coaching others to world titles. I'd done all that they'd asked, played by all the rules, done all the right things.

"Traitor! Spy! Disgrace! *Capitalist!*" The words hit like red-hot irons jabbed into my stomach, leaving behind agony but no physical injury. Then I was grabbed and dragged off the platform by the Red Guards, mostly university students with red bands on their arms. They took me to a nearby house, which I

The Spirit of Pong

somehow recognized as mine, and threw me into a room. Before closing the door, a man with a high, screechy voice lectured me.

"You believe the purpose of sport is to obtain titles, showing an impurity of thought. You are guilty of trophyism. You will stay here until you are absolved of this revisionist thinking. You will begin by reading the required text." Then he slammed the door. I heard the door click.

The room was nearly bare, with just a small bed, and a small table and chair. A bucket sat in a corner. An old jump rope lay on the floor. Overhead was a dim light fixture. On the table was a little red book, *The Quotations of Mao Zedong*.

At first I ignored it. But there literally wasn't anything else to do in the tiny room, other than perhaps do some of the physical training exercises that Ogimura had taught me, or think over some of the things Rong had taught me. And so I finally picked it up to read.

But Ogimura had taught me that if I wanted to be a champion, I had to eat, drink, and breathe table tennis. And so I put it down, and resolved not to open it. Instead, I increased my table tennis training and thinking. I jumped rope, often hours at a time. I went over everything I had learned from Rong, often arguing and re-arguing the finer points. With his absence, I even won some of the arguments.

Once every night the door would open, and the Red Guards would return. They would silently handcuff me, and two would hold me down while another beat me with a stick.

"Do you repent your thinking?" shouted one. "Tell us why what you did was wrong!" I would ignore him. Then they would leave just as silently, only to return the following night to repeat the routine.

The screechy-voice man hadn't been entirely accurate when he'd said I would stay in the room until I was "absolved of this revisionist thinking." Every few days the Red Guards dragged me through the streets, put me on the platform, and the crowds pelted me with rocks and insults. I was ordered to "Tell us why what you did was wrong," but I remained silent.

A pain built up in my head as this went on, day after day, week after week, month after month. I hadn't marked off the days as I had with Ogimura and Rong, having no writing

The Spirit of Pong

utensils, and so lost track of time. The pain became unbearable. The beatings grew worse, but the pain in my head, the agony of humiliation, was far worse.

One day they stopped locking the door from the outside, and I was apparently free to go. But where was I supposed to go? I wandered the streets, wondering what to do. The country I had known was no longer my country, with Red Guards everywhere. Every few days I was still forced to march through the streets, often wearing signs proclaiming my crimes. The beatings continued every night.

One morning I found myself staring at the jump rope. Then I touched the birthmark on my neck. The mark of a rope, Coach Wang had said. It had been a few days since they had last paraded me on the platform; they would probably drag me out again tomorrow. I grabbed the jump rope and walked through the local area until I came to a tree with a large branch perhaps ten feet from the ground. I hung myself, and my pain was over.

I lay on the ground next to the grave of Rong Guotuan. I clutched clods of dirt tightly in each hand. All my muscles were tensed and my neck hurt. I could smell the fresh earth in the bright afternoon sun. Then I relaxed the muscles, dropping the clods of dirt.

And suddenly my mind was clear. Truly clear, for the first time in my life. My eyes went wide even as my brain flew free of whatever had held it back all these years. It flowed freely over the past, like a videotape played in reverse at one hundred, no, one thousand times normal speed. My mind zipped past to my recent loss at the USA Nationals and all the tactical errors I'd made and how little my mind had been prepared for combat. Why, even on the last point how had I missed how Derek Klaus Hsu had been leaning back when I got ready to smack in that forehand that he'd counter-smash to win—a simple soft block to his forehand would have left him flailing.

Then the same for every match I'd ever played, like a ten-thousand-hour movie played in a minute.

"This is incredible!" I cried as I stood up. I looked at Coach Wang, and once again he smiled.

"How long have I been gone?" I asked.

The Spirit of Pong

"Five minutes." He pointed at me with his ever-present cigarette. "You now have the Body of Pong and the Mind of Pong. Now you must achieve the third secret of Pong."

I felt invincible. How could there be anything else?

"And what is that?"

"You must get the Paddle of Pong."

Little did I know that this next task would be the most difficult and dangerous of all.

The Spirit of Pong

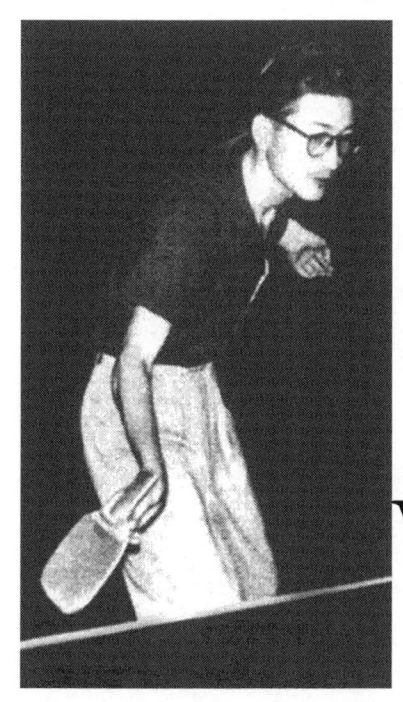

Chapter 7
The Paddle of Pong

We flew northeast that very night to Shanghai, 800 miles away on the east coast of China, on the East China Sea, facing Japan. We arrived late that night, and spent the night at a hotel, with Coach Wang paying. The following morning we called a taxi and we soon stood in front of the Double Happiness Table Tennis Company, one of the largest and most famous table tennis companies in the world. They made all types of equipment—tables, balls, rackets, and the modern inverted sponges that covered the rackets and allowed modern players to put so much spin on their shots.

The company was created in 1959 by the Chinese government, and was named Double Happiness by Premier Zhou Enlai to celebrate the double happiness from the tenth anniversary of the Communist takeover of China in 1949, and, ironically, for Rong Guotuan's win in men's singles at the 1959 World Championships, nine years before his 1968 suicide—with Zhou Enlai still Premier.

"What do we do now?" I asked.

"It is not what *we* do," Coach Wang said. "Did I go in with you to train with Ogimura? Did I go with you to learn from Rong? You did those things on your own, and you now have the Body of Pong and the Mind of Pong. And now you must complete your training and get the Paddle of Pong."

The Spirit of Pong

I'd never been an equipment junky, one of those players in constant search of the "perfect" equipment, with some believing that if they got just the right combination it might make them a champion. I could beat most of those players using a book as a racket. And yet, there had always been rumors that the great Chinese champions had a secret weapon in their paddles. Apparently they did.

"So how do I get this Paddle of Pong?"

"You must go inside, to the vault, alone, and there you must face . . . the Dragon."

"You mean Ma Long, the 2015 men's singles world champion? Don't they call him the Dragon?"

Coach Wang smiled. "For him it is only a nickname. I speak of one from long ago, one who is far more ferocious."

I'd faced many adversaries in my table tennis life, but all had normal names. *The Dragon?* Considering what I'd gone through so far, with my luck it would literally be a dragon.

"So who is 'the Dragon'?"

"I have practiced with him many times," said Coach Wang, a faraway look in his eyes as he stared at the entrance. And was that a tear? But Coach Wang wiped whatever it was away. "That is all I can say."

"Can't you come in with me?"

"*No!*" he thundered. I'd never seen him lose his temper quite like that—sort of a mixture of anger, fear, and stark terror. There was more to this than he was saying.

"If I must face the Dragon, can't you at least tell me something about him? And what exactly will we be doing, facing each other? Is it like a staring contest?"

Coach Wang took several deep breaths. "He is the most dangerous player you will ever meet. You will play him, and you will either come out with the Paddle of Pong, or you will not come out alive."

I couldn't tell if he was being literal or mystical. Ogimura had nearly worked me to death, but I don't think I had ever been literally in danger of my life. Rong had put me through the tortures he had faced and his suicide, but it had all been in my head, and I don't think my life had ever actually been in danger.

The Spirit of Pong

"You want me to risk my life for a piece of table tennis equipment?"

"I want you to risk your life to become a champion. Without the Paddle of Pong, you are nothing."

Was it worth it? I wasn't sure. But what had Ogimura said? *"If you want to be champion, you must be willing to die for it."* I wasn't sure if the real Ogimura had said that, but the spirit of whatever made him champion had said it.

I had come to China to learn the secrets of Chinese table tennis, and I was two-thirds there. I couldn't stop now. I *must* have the Paddle of Pong.

"So what do I do? Break in through a window? Stand over a grave? Or just go up and knock?"

Coach Wang laughed. "This time it is rather easy. Put on your playing shoes, and take your racket with you. Then just go up and knock. Ask for the tour. At some point during the tour they will take you through the part of the factory where they make the rackets themselves. While there you will see a small, black door in the back. Hide until the rest have left, and then go to that door. It will be locked, but the combination to the lock is 1-9-5-2. It opens into The Vault. And there you will meet the Dragon."

"How do you know the combination?"

"I was there. Ask no more questions until you have returned."

And so I found myself on the tour, seeing how they made the tables, the balls, the sponges, and finally the rackets. Considering my life centered on table tennis, it now seemed rather surprising to me that I had never really learned how any of these things were made. Much of it was automated, but everything was hand inspected before it was sent out for distribution.

There was the machine that created the new seamless balls. They wouldn't let us see it up close—trade secrets—but we saw vats of melted plastic go in, and ping-pong balls come out.

We saw huge squares of yellow, orange, blue, and other colored table tennis sponge baking to the proper characteristics, and equally huge squares of black or red pimpled rubber come

The Spirit of Pong

out of molds. And then we saw them as they were placed together, and then cut into the familiar seven-inch squares, and then machine packaged, ready for delivery.

We saw rackets being machine made, with thin ply sheets stuck together and then cut into the proper shape, and then the two small parts of the handle glued on, all automated.

While the guide lectured on about racket production—I had no idea what she was saying since it was in Chinese—I spied the small, black door. The Vault. When no one was looking I ducked down under a table, suddenly realizing how silly I'd look if they found me, and also realizing that maybe, being the only non-Chinese person in the group, they might quickly note my absence. But the group continued the tour, and I quickly made my way to the door.

The combination 1-9-5-2 worked on the first try, and the door opened. I stooped and stepped inside.

Because he'd called it a vault, I'd assumed it would be a small room. But the brightly-lit room was rather large—in fact, I quickly realized it was about fourteen by seven meters, the size of a professional table tennis court. And sitting in the middle of it was a Double Happiness ping-pong table.

The room had the same red rubberized floor and green walls as the Chinese National Training Center gym. Portraits lined the walls. I approached them and realized they were pictures of past world champions, men and women, going back to the first world championships in 1926.

"You wish to play for the Paddle of Pong?" I jumped at the unexpected words—I thought I'd been alone. Sitting in a chair next to the table was a slight man with glasses. He sat so still I hadn't noticed him. By his feet was a hexagon-shaped wooden box about the size of a bowling ball, covered in intricate carvings.

The man stood. He was a thin yet tall wisp of a man, dressed in black shirt and shorts, and like Ogimura and Rong, slightly translucent. He began to wipe his glasses with a small cloth. I did a double take, but there was no question about the identity of the Japanese man who in 1952 had changed the sport forever and brought it into the modern age by winning men's singles at the World Championships using a sponge racket.

The Spirit of Pong

Before that nearly everyone covered their racket with plain "pimpled" rubber. But Hiroji Satoh had died in 2000; like Ogimura, every serious player remembers where he was when he first heard. He was looking at me as if waiting for something, and then I remembered he'd asked a question.

"Yes, I wish to play for the Paddle of Pong. Are you the Dragon?"

He nodded. "Let us begin. We will play one game to 11. Would you like to serve or receive?"

"Receive."

He nodded. "I'm guessing you learned that from Ogimura or Rong. I think it was their turn to teach."

"Yes," I said. "Body of Pong, Mind of Pong, it's all here."

"So said Coach Wang, standing where you are now."

"He was *here?*"

"He did not tell you?" Satoh smiled. "I know all about him. He had Body of Pong and Mind of Pong. He trained very hard, but Ogimura and Rong told me they weren't so impressed with his character. Neither was I. He played me for the Paddle of Pong."

"Since he's alive, he must have defeated you," I pointed out.

"He did not," said Satoh. "It was good battle, but I beat him, 11-6. Don't you know? *I was his coach.* A coach knows his student's game, so student can never defeat his coach. We both knew he had no chance. I think he hoped to steal Paddle of Pong. Which is why I now keep them locked up." He gestured at a safe sitting in the corner. "I promise you combination to that isn't as predictable as 1-9-5-2."

Satoh was Coach Wang's coach? *Why hadn't he told me?* But there was something wrong here.

"I thought whoever loses to you dies?" I asked.

"They do," said Satoh. "But he showed poor character. When he lost, he ran for door and was out before I could flame him."

"Flame him?"

Satoh smiled. "You have much to learn. But now I keep doors locked while we play." He held up a small device and

51

The Spirit of Pong

pushed a button. There was a click from the door. "Nobody leaves until our business is complete. We will now warm up for two minutes, and then we will play."

"You get to use the Paddle of Pong while I get stuck with a normal one?"

Satoh grinned. "I would never take such unfair advantage. But if you wish to be a Champion, you must learn to play anything." He leaned over and took the lid off of the hexagonal box by his feet, and pulled out . . . something.

It was a huge hexagonal mallet, sort of like a six-sided spin top or Jewish dreidel, with each side the size of a ping-pong paddle's playing surface, each a different color. A thick handle stuck out the top, seemingly far too big for human hands. Satoh, who used the penhold grip, gripped the too-big handle awkwardly like it was chopsticks, with the hitting surface below, a common grip in Asia. Satoh held the racket out and slowly spun it in front of me, like a giant upside-down club. It had six of the most common surfaces in table tennis.

The red surface was a tensored inverted sponge, with a smooth and grippy surface, by far the most popular surface among top players, and the surface I used on both sides of my paddle. It practically grabbed the ball and shot it out with speed and spin. It was mostly used to attack with lots of topspin, a loop drive. Since it created the most spin, it was also the best surface for creating spinny serves.

The orange was pips-out sponge, excellent for quick blocking and smashing. Spin didn't affect it as much as inverted, and its shots also didn't have as much spin as inverted, though more than the other surfaces.

The green was hardbat, just like pips-out sponge but without the sponge. It was rarely used anymore except in specialized hardbat events, not since Satoh's introduction of the sponge surface, but it was good for ball control, defense, and smashing if the ball didn't have too much topspin.

The blue was antispin, a unique type of smooth inverted sponge where the sponge was slow and the surface slippery, so that spin didn't take on it. It was excellent for returning spin, but was only good for defense, and couldn't create much spin on its own.

The Spirit of Pong

The yellow and purple were both long pips surfaces, where the pips were extra long and soft, and so bent when hit by the ball. The yellow one had sponge under it, and was designed for backspin defense from away from the table. The purple one had no sponge under it, and was designed for backspin defense from close to the table, where you contacted the ball quick off the bounce. Both were defensive surfaces, designed to return the opponent's own spin, thereby forcing him to deal with his own spin. They returned topspin as backspin, and backspin as topspin, causing opponents great difficulty as they faced their own returning spins. Long pips without sponge was especially diabolical, returning the maximum amount of an attacker's spins right back at him just by sticking the racket out.

I'd known the basics on how to play all of these surfaces before I'd come to China, and Rong had drilled into me the higher intricacies of each. While most top players use tensored inverted sponge on both sides, some use one of these alternate surfaces on the other, to befuddle an opponent who has to adjust to two different surfaces—especially if the player learns to flip his racket so he can use either surface on forehand or backhand. But I was used to facing no more than two surfaces at a time, always red and black by the rules—now I was faced with six surfaces, with six colors to keep track of!

Satoh and I started to hit. One of the stranger traditions in table tennis is the two-minute warm-up. The purpose is to allow both players to get warmed up, but it means you are equally warming up your opponent, the person you are trying to beat. It makes more sense to warm up *before* the match, with someone else, than to go to the table to hit for two minutes, where half the point is to help out your opponent. But it's tradition—and in this case, the warm-up probably favored me, as I had just flown 800 miles, taken a taxi, and walked around in a long tour. It would have helped to hit against each of the six surfaces on Satoh's racket, but he warmed up only with the tensored inverted. It did give me a glimpse into his style. He had a rather short stroke, and I remembered hearing that he was mostly a blocker with a somewhat efficient forehand smash. But the spirits of Ogimura and Rong had both expanded their table tennis skills since their deaths, and so perhaps had Satoh. For

The Spirit of Pong

one thing, I doubt if the living Satoh—or anyone else—had ever used a six-sided paddle. The unwieldy racket seemed far too big and heavy for this slight and meek-looking man, like a small child waving a giant troll's battle club. How could he have struck fear into players, much less win the world championships?

"Time!" said Satoh. "Now we truly begin." I paused to remove my warm-up pants, and took a few deep breaths to relax.

He began by serving with the red surface, the grippy, tensored inverted, which by far gave the most spin. It was a short backspin serve, just over the net and short to my forehand, so I had to reach in to return it.

And that's when Satoh, known as the Dragon, expanded into a dragon. *A real one.*

Chapter 8
The Dragon

It was an Asian-style dragon, more serpentine than the dinosaur types often depicted in the U.S. and Europe. Unlike the slightly translucent Satoh, it looked completely solid. It was wingless and bright red, with a yellow belly, with yellow the color of royalty in China, courage in Japan. Red and blue tendrils came out of its head and back. Its mouth was open, showing huge, yellow teeth. It stood on its back legs, which would have put its head perhaps twelve feet in the air, but it was hunched over down to table level, clutching the giant hexagonal paddle in its front right claws. Now the racket looked like a toy in the grip of this giant monster. Stretched out I'm guessing it would have been about twenty feet long.

  I took all this in while I reflexively pushed his serve back with my own backspin, but no longer paying close attention, I returned it weakly toward his backhand side. The dragon stepped over, and ripped a forehand loop from its backhand side for a winner that I didn't even react to—I was gaping at the dragon.

The Spirit of Pong

Only it was no longer a dragon; the instant the point ended it shrank back down to the meek-looking Satoh. He smiled; 1-0.

It did not matter that my opponent was a dragon. I needed to focus. Where did his glasses go when he transformed? No, forget that; concentrate. He'd just looped a winner past me. Satoh during his heyday never had such a topspin shot, which only a few people experimented with in the 1950s, and wasn't really developed until the 1960s. Obviously he had been learning as a spirit. I would have to be ready. Even if I hadn't been caught off guard by Satoh's transformation I would likely have lost the point. He'd attacked it right at my elbow, where I would have had to make an instant decision on whether to take it forehand or backhand, which is difficult against an aggressive shot like Satoh's loop.

We both knew this was a learning experience, and I had just learned several things about him. In a best of five or best of seven match, I could afford to lose the first game to learn about the opponent's game, but not here, in a single game to eleven.

Once again Satoh served with the red inverted, this time short to my backhand, and once again he transformed into the dragon as soon as the ball was in play, as he would the entire game. His serve gave me an angle into his wide backhand. But what had Rong said about doing the obvious? I faked another deep backspin return to his backhand, and at the last second changed and pushed it deep to the forehand. Sure enough, the dragon had started to step around its backhand again. It quickly changed directions and managed to make a weak topspin shot with the inverted side. I prepared to attack it.

Fire shot at me from the dragon's mouth. After the initial shock of the dragon, somehow I was ready and ducked, and the fire went over my head. I got up instantly, and topspinned the ball back to its backhand, and prepared for a weaker backhand return. But the dragon twirled its racket like a top, and blocked it with the purple side. Which surface was that? Unsure, I patted the ball back, straight into the net. The purple side was the long pips without sponge, and so it had returned all my topspin as backspin, leading to my mistake. Once again the dragon turned into a smiling Satoh; 2-0.

The Spirit of Pong

Now it was my serve. I served short to the forehand with heavy sidespin, with Satoh transforming into the dragon as I did so. It dropped the ball short with the blue side with a downward stroke, meaning backspin. At the last second, as I ducked another flame, I realized that was the antispin, and so its return had little spin. But I was too late—I reached over the table and attacked it with my backhand, but thinking the ball had more backspin, I lifted it off the end. Before transforming back the dragon roared, and shot fire off to the side, charring the wall. Then it transformed back to a smiling Satoh; 3-0.

I stepped back off the table. I wouldn't have a chance if I couldn't keep track of the surfaces, even as I ducked its flames. And so I called a one-minute time-out, which you are allowed to do once per match. Satoh frowned for a second; there was no such thing as a time-out in his day. I had sixty seconds, and I had to make them count. I said to myself: red—inverted; orange—pips-out; green—hardbat; blue—antispin; yellow—long pips with sponge; purple—long pips without sponge.

But memorizing the words wasn't good enough; it had to be instinctive. I needed mnemonic devices to remember them. Red is red hot, like the red-hot topspin attack of tensored inverted. Orange is fiery, like a pips-out smash. Green is the color of nature, and hardbat was the natural surface of table tennis for much of its history. Blue is the color of calm, like an antispin return without spin. Yellow is like the sun, far away, like far-off backspin defense of long pips with sponge. Purple is the color of mystery, like the mysterious returns of long pips without sponge as they return nearly all of your own spin.

I was ready for its surfaces, but was I ready for the dragon? I would have to rely on my Ogimura-training to avoid the flames. I glanced up; Satoh was wiping his glasses.

"Time," Satoh said a moment later as he put his glasses back on. I returned to the table.

He'd be expecting another short serve, I thought, and may use the same surface or another. So I decided to cross him up. I served fast topspin to his deep backhand—and it did catch the dragon off guard. Against a deep serve it's best to topspin with inverted, a loop, but it had been planning to return my expected short, spinny serve with its purple side, the color of

The Spirit of Pong

mystery, which I now instantly recognized as the long pips no sponge. I knew I'd get my topspin back as a backspin, which came to my backhand. I wound up, and did a powerful backhand loop right down the line to its forehand side. As I did so it flamed me, this time catching me full on the chest. My shirt burst into flame. I dropped my paddle and brushed out the flames. As I did so, it stretched out its full serpentine length, trying to reach my shot, but it was not fast enough as my shot went for an ace. Satoh reappeared, now stretched out on the floor. He rose, and brushed off his clothes. Then he glanced at me and nodded; 3-1.

My shirt was now a blackened crisp, with most of the front gone. My chest was as bright red as the dragon. I ignored the pain.

It was now an equal battle, now that I had the surfaces down. We battled on and on, the dragon twirling its war club like Darth Maul and his double-sided light saber in *Star Wars*, flaming me at key times during the rallies, and with me using serves and serve returns to set up my relentless topspin attacks. My shirt was pretty much gone, and my shorts were mostly burned away as well.

Soon he led 9-7, Satoh to serve. He had been serving with the red inverted throughout, but now he tried to catch me off guard by serving fast and deep with the orange short pips, barely getting the serve off before transforming into the dragon. Knowing the ball would have less spin than its previous serves, I adjusted and made a powerful backhand loop to its wide backhand, barely ducking a flame as I did so. But it had stepped off the table and chopped it back with the yellow side, which meant long pips with sponge. It would be extremely heavy backspin, far more than the backspin off a topspin serve. If I tried attacking, I'd likely miss or make a weak shot. Instead, I took it right off the bounce and pushed it with backspin right back to its wide backhand. It had twirled his racket and returned it with the green side, the side of nature, the hardbat. This gave it control, but not a lot of backspin on its return. As I wound up for a big forehand, it caught me full in the face with a flame, blinding me. But I'd already timed the shot, and I let it go. I

The Spirit of Pong

didn't see, but heard the winner go down the line as I pulled to 9-8.

I stepped back, trying to clear my eyes. After a moment my vision returned, though I could feel that my eyebrows had been burned away, along with some of my hair.

Next Satoh served short backspin to the middle of the table. This was dangerous; from the middle of the table there's no wide angle to play into, and so any deep return would likely give it a forehand attack. I aimed to its wide backhand, but instead did a quick backspin push to its wide forehand. But the dragon and was ready, and did a powerful forehand loop with its red inverted. I blocked it back weakly toward its backhand, but it had already stepped over and smashed it to my wide backhand with the fiery orange side, the pips-out, the best surface for smashing. I saw it coming, and raced backwards, and was able to lob it back high, almost to the ceiling fifteen feet over us, with some topspin. But it smashed it again to my wide backhand, and again I lobbed. It's one of my strengths, but it's a difficult way to win a point. Then it smashed to my forehand. I raced over and counter-smashed—the training with Ogimura had dramatically increased my speed. But the dragon stuck its racket out and dead-blocked the ball back with the blue antispin, the slowest of surfaces, and I could only watch as the ball bounced three times on my side of the table. Once again the dragon roared, and this time it flamed the entire wall to its left, turning it into a black cinder, but somehow the wall held. It transformed back, and Satoh smiled; 10-8 game point.

"I am sorry for what I must soon do," said Satoh. "Your death will be quick and merciful."

There's no more pressure than being down 10-8 and facing a quick and merciful death, except perhaps facing a more painful one. So I was glad I had given the serve away at the start so I'd be serving at the end. But what to serve? And how to prepare for its varied shots and surfaces?

Then it struck me that all along Satoh, or the dragon, had been controlling the rallies. I was faster, with more powerful shots, and yet we were playing even because the dragon was in control while I was just reacting to its shots.

The Spirit of Pong

"Observe the habits of your opponent," Rong had said. And there were patterns to its play. When it attacked with the red inverted, it almost always followed by smashing with the orange short pips. When I attacked and it was close to the table, it defended with the purple long pips no sponge, while if it was off the table it defended with the yellow long pips with sponge. When it wanted to put the ball very short it mostly used the blue antispin. When it wanted a pure control shot, it mostly used the green hardbat. Tactics is maximizing your chances of winning, so why wasn't I maximizing my chances of winning by taking advantage of this predictableness?

I served short to its forehand even as Satoh transformed. It would want to keep the ball short and low to stop my loop, and so would likely return with antispin, as it had done before. Sure enough, it dropped it short with the blue side—but I was ready for this spinless ball, and snapped in a backhand winner before it even had a chance to shoot flames. Once again Satoh nodded; 10-9.

If I served short to its backhand again, it would likely cross me up with a different surface; it wasn't about to use the antispin again. So I served fast to its backhand. As I did so, it engulfed me in flames, and I could barely see the dragon. I ignored the heat and somehow kept my eyes open, and caught a glimpse of the dragon as it returned my serve. I had guessed right; it returned it with the red inverted, a quick block to my wide backhand. But I was ready, and I backhand looped it right back to its backhand, pinning it down there. The advantage of my shakehands grip is a stronger backhand attack then a penholder with a conventional backhand like Satoh, who was forced to block. It stayed with the inverted, with a quick block to my backhand, followed by a burst of flame that I successfully ducked. But I knew it was just a matter of time before it twirled to the long pips no sponge, so I attacked again to its backhand, but without too much topspin—and sure enough, it had twirled to the mysterious purple. I stepped over, and since my shot hadn't had too much topspin, its return didn't have too much backspin. I ripped a winner to its wide forehand. Satoh frowned; 10-all.

The Spirit of Pong

Now it was his serve. Satoh had been mostly serving short to my forehand or long to my backhand; I prepared to move diagonally to either. I watched him serve with the red inverted side, and saw a little extra backswing—which meant he was likely serving long. I began to step around to attack the deep serve to my backhand with my forehand. But he'd crossed me up, and the serve went down the line to my forehand. Everything seemed to slow down as I fought to recover and change directions in an instant as I watched the ball on its way toward an ace winner.

But I had trained with Ogimura for a year. My legs were like a cheetah's. I sprang back to my right, and with a big shoulder rotation, ripped a forehand loop down the line right back at the dragon. Caught off guard, and reflexively moving to cover its open forehand side, it could only stare at my shot as it went by; 11-10 me.

Now I served for the game. Should I go for a conventional serve, and hope to get a return I could attack? Or should I be a bit more tactical? I thought it over, and then I smiled for the first time. Satoh had had the right idea in serving fast to my forehand, just the wrong opponent.

I faked a deep serve to the backhand, just as Satoh had done to me. But he had many more decades of experience than I did, and had probably studied my serving motion during the game, and so didn't fall for it; the dragon was ready with a big inverted loop. But it didn't matter; I quick-blocked the ball to the middle of the table, which gave it another forehand but cut off any wide angles. Then I took a half step back, and prepared.

As I expected, it had switched to the orange short-pips to smash. Anticipating this allowed me to react to its fiery smash, even as it simultaneously shot out a fiery burst of flame. Before his shot even crossed the net I was already moving into position, timing it just right against the pips-out smash, which has less topspin than an inverted smash. Both the smash and the flames were coming to my backhand corner. The year of Ogimura training allowed me to step over and throw my whole body into my forehand counter-smash to his wide backhand. I saw the dragon lunge for the ball, but then I disappeared into the flames.

The Spirit of Pong

I nearly somersaulted through them, landing on and scraping my hands and knees.

The dragon was staring at the ball, which now lay against the far wall. Had my shot hit?

Then it transformed back into Satoh, who looked like he'd seen a ghost. Then a forced smile came over his face, and he stepped toward me, extending his hand. "Good game. Ogimura and Rong have trained you well." He bowed.

I bowed back, trying to ignore the painful burns and scraped hands and knees. "You have improved since 1952."

"Many hours practicing with Ogimura, Rong, Zhuang Zedong, and others." He pulled off his glasses and began to wipe them. After a moment he put them back on. "You have won a Paddle of Pong. Guard it well."

Something seemed wrong. Coach Wang had always referred to it as "The Paddle of Pong," so I had assumed there was only one. Now I realized that couldn't be right—after all, wouldn't the Chinese team members all have Paddles of Pong? Or did they?

"How many are there?"

"As many as needed," said Satoh. He bent down to the safe in the corner, put in the combination, and soon held up a simple, unmarked blue paddle case. He removed the paddle from it and handed it to me. The racket seemed to have an aura about it—and then I realized it literally did have an aura, with a very faint light emanating from all sides. It was plain wood, covered by an unlabeled sponge surface, red on one side, black on the other, as required.

"You have earned this," Satoh said. He looked me up and down, but politely didn't comment on my state of undress, with my shirt completely burned away and my shorts in tatters. "Beware relying on equipment—it can only take you so far, as it took me to only one championship. It is only one ingredient. Now you may leave." He clicked to unlock the door. Then he bowed, and returned to the chair by the table, where he sat and seemed to meditate.

As I left, he called out to me, "We will meet again. Soon."

The Spirit of Pong

During the tour we had visited the Double Happiness clothing store. I sneaked my way back, and I'm sorry to say, stole some badly needed table tennis clothing to replace the charred remains of my own. Someday I'd pay them back.

Chapter 9
Shanghai Shock

"I won!" I cried, holding up the Paddle of Pong. The shiny black and red surfaces reflected brightly in the late morning sunlight like the red and black flag of Albania. I'd once defeated a member of their national team, one of my greatest moments, but nothing could compare to this. I now had my weapon, a mighty harpoon to capture the whale.

"You now have the Body, Mind, and Paddle of Pong," Coach Wang said, smiling more brightly then I'd ever seen him. He was twirling his cigarette in his hand in seeming excitement.

Somehow I couldn't imagine him the way Satoh had described him, trying to steal the Paddle of Pong, and scurrying out the door when he lost. He had led me through this whole process, and he, along with Ogimura, Rong, and Satoh, would always be my heroes, the ones who had made it all possible. Now my training was complete; it was time to return to America and make the National Team so I could compete at the upcoming World Championships. I'd seen the Chinese National Team; they had grown fat and lazy. Through their Sweat of Champions they may still have the Body of Pong, but mine was fresher, and they would never have my drive. I would defeat them and be World Champion. There was no doubt in my mind.

The Spirit of Pong

"Let's celebrate," I said. "What's the best restaurant in Shanghai?"

"We will go to the Din Tai Fung, which is nearby," said Coach Wang. "They make the best dumplings in China."

I felt in a dreamland as we took the taxi to the restaurant for lunch. I felt like I had spent nearly three years in China—a year with Ogimura, a year with Rong, and who knows how long reliving the Cultural Revolution with Rong. In reality, I had been here barely a day and a half. I'd arrived at sundown the day before yesterday, where I'd met up with Coach Wang. At midnight I'd broken into the Chinese National Training Center. I'd finished my training with Ogimura the following morning. We'd flown to Zhuhai City that afternoon, where I'd learned from Rong and faced the Red Guards. We'd flown to Shanghai that night, and I'd played Satoh the following morning—this morning. And yet, I was a changed man, in body and mind. I clutched the Paddle of Pong tightly to my chest as we drove through the Shanghai streets.

Coach Wang ordered the dumplings, and spent several minutes explaining in graphic detail just how good they would be.

"But you have just played the Dragon," he said. "You are a sweaty mess. Go to the restroom and get cleaned up."

I looked down at myself—he was right. I had sweated through the new Double Happiness clothing. My hands also felt grimy with sweat. I was burned all over—it was starting to really sting.

"I'll be right back!" Off I went. I was gone less than five minutes. When I returned, Coach Wang was gone. His still-burning cigarette lay in an ash tray.

Also gone was the Paddle of Pong.

I waved my arm at the nearest waitress, probably a bit too much as people stared, but I didn't care. "Miss, did you see where the man with me went?"

"He left, carrying that blue ping-pong paddle case," she said. "He seemed in a big rush."

I hailed a cab, and then remembered I didn't have any money, as I'd already explained to the disgruntled waitress when

The Spirit of Pong

I'd been forced to cancel our orders. I tried explaining my situation to the cab driver, but I couldn't even tell if he understood my English as he shook his head and drove off. I tried several more times, to no avail. Finally I sat on the curb. What was I to do?

It all seemed so obvious now. According to Satoh, Coach Wang had gotten the Body of Pong and the Mind of Pong. But he had also said a student could never defeat his coach, and since Satoh had been Coach Wang's coach, Coach Wang could never get a Paddle of Pong. And so he had resorted to trickery—training me, or at least getting Ogimura and Rong to do so, in the hopes that I could get a Paddle of Pong. And then he stole it, and left me penniless on the streets of Shanghai. I'd come to China to learn the secrets of Chinese table tennis so I could become a champion, and instead I had been the instrument for Coach Wang to do so.

The Double Happiness Company was less than two miles away, so I walked back. When I asked to see Mr. Satoh, they looked at me like I was crazy. So I went on another tour, and ended up at the door to the Vault again. Once again 1-9-5-2 let me in.

He was waiting for me. "I told you we would meet again soon," said Satoh. "Let me guess. Coach Wang stole your Paddle of Pong?"

"It was that obvious?"

"Yes."

"Why didn't you tell me?"

"Would you have believed me?" I started to answer, but realized he was right.

"So what do I do now? Do I have to play you again? I don't think I could survive that."

"No, you would not," said Satoh, who was suddenly the Dragon, nonchalantly flaming the walls again. And then he transformed back. "And even if you did, you only get one chance at it. You can never win another Paddle of Pong. And so Coach Wang will likely win the World Championships. Unless you stop him."

"And how do I do that without a Paddle of Pong?"

The Spirit of Pong

"With this." Satoh held a small, worn-out brown box that looked ancient, apparently a racket case. "It is yours now."

I took the case and opened it; the hinges creaked as I did so. If the racket case looked old, the racket inside was far worse, the most dilapidated, worn-out paddle I had ever seen. It was a penhold blade, with a square hitting surface, and thick, yellow sponge that looked about seven millimeters thick, over a quarter inch. And then I realized that, like the other Paddle of Pong, it too had that very light, barely noticeable aura of light coming out of it.

"You want me to play with *this*?"

"It is the paddle I used in 1952," Satoh explained. "It is first Paddle of Pong. It was mine, but now it is yours."

I stared at the beat-up thing. It may have been top-of-the-line in 1952, when it was the only sponge racket in use by the top players, but now it was a piece of junk. Plus there were some technical difficulties.

"It's a penhold blade," I pointed out. "I'm a shakehander. The handle is too short and is shaped for a penholder."

Satoh smiled. "It is Paddle of Pong. You must trust it."

"The sponge is too thick, and doesn't have a rubber covering. No umpire or referee would allow it." The sponge and rubber on each side of the racket cannot be more than four millimeters, and plain sponge without rubber isn't legal.

"Are you sure?"

"And it looks pretty worn out."

"Is it?"

I continued to stare at it. Suddenly it hit me—I was holding the actual racket Satoh had won with, the racket that changed history! It was like holding the Magna Carta or George Washington's false teeth, only better, since it was table tennis.

"This is the greatest gift ever," I said. "I don't know how to thank you!"

"Just beat Coach Wang," said Satoh. "I really don't like him."

"I will!" I exclaimed.

Satoh shook his head. "His name brings back bad memories. Coach Wang very ambitious man. But he have big

The Spirit of Pong

head, and dishonest, so nobody in China would coach him. So he come to Japan. They quickly learn about him, and soon nobody there would coach him either. So I coach him. Big mistake."

It did seem unfair that Coach Wang's coach had been the very person he'd need to beat to get a Paddle of Pong, but he'd brought that on himself when every other coach had refused him. I wasn't going to feel sorry for him. Now that I had a Paddle of Pong, I knew what I must do. The whale was mine.

"I will beat him for you. I even know a little about how he plays, from back when he was coaching me before he—"

"What did you say?" interrupted Satoh. "Did you say he coach you?"

Suddenly it dawned on me. "It was only one session, just before he sent me to Ogimura."

"Did you accept him as your coach?"

"Well, yes, he asked me that specifically."

Satoh was shaking his head. "It doesn't matter. There was a reason he did that before sending you to Ogimura, to remove you as possible threat. A coach knows your game, and so you can never defeat your coach."

It took a moment for that to sink in. I'm not sure how long I stood there, frozen and unable to move, just staring, first at Satoh, and then off into space. But there was no mistaking his words. The realities of championship table tennis were harsh.

And so my quest was over. Regaining a Paddle of Pong had been pointless. And my trip to China had been pointless. The great whale I sought was slowly sinking out of my grasp.

"You may keep paddle," said Satoh. "I always felt bad about beating American Marty Reisman at 1952 Worlds. He had much promise as hardbat player, but sponge destroyed him. You may not win Worlds, but you can be greatest American player in history and second greatest in world to newest Chinese star."

Chapter 10
Back to America

Mr. Satoh was a great man, or at least a great spirit. Knowing my predicament, he paid my way back to America. Later I wondered how a spirit had cash on hand, but why not? And so I returned to the Maryland Table Tennis Center. Perhaps with the help of my Body of Pong, I healed quickly from the burns I'd received in my match with Satoh. When I had left, I had been a second-tier American player with hopes to be the best in the world. Now I was one of the very best players in the world, but with no hopes to be the best.

I could go over the details of what happened at the USA Team Trials at Caesars Palace in Las Vegas, but they would be tedious and repetitive. The short version—I killed everyone, finishing first, winning every match 4-0. The games were to 11; I never gave up more than five points in a game. When I played my old rival and U.S. champion Derek Klaus Hsu, I won 11-2, 11-4, 11-5, 11-1. In the last game I was up 10-0 and played a "mercy" lobbing point which entertained the crowd and allowed him to save face. Now that I could beat him he didn't seem like such a bad guy.

The strangest part was Satoh's racket. When I went out to play my first match with this obviously illegal racket, I was a bit nervous. How could I win with such a paddle? But like Satoh transforming into a dragon at the beginning of each point, the

The Spirit of Pong

instant the point began—or whenever an umpire or referee tried to examine it—the paddle transformed into a shakehand racket with tensored inverted sponge. As soon as the point ended—or a person examining it gave it back to me—it transformed back to the original dilapidated penhold version. I heard the TV commentators and officials were going crazy seeing this, but what could they do?

Before each match I drank a few drops of the Sweat of Champions, those cases of my sweat that Ogimura had so carefully mopped up and saved for me. I studied my opponent's game before each match, and applied the tactics I had learned from Rong, all part of the Mind of Pong.

In the U.S., I was famous, at least in the table tennis world—which, of course, isn't really that big. But worldwide, few noticed. How could they, when everyone was watching the rise of the newest Chinese star, a relative unknown before, who went by the rather unlikely name of . . . Coach Wang. Table tennis might not be big in the U.S., but it's huge overseas, and so Coach Wang quickly became an international star. Traveling on the World Tour he won event after event—the Japan Open, Korean Open, Australian Open, English Open, Swedish Open, German Open, Hungarian Open, Polish Open, Kuwait Open, and the Qatar Open. Each time he took home prize money over a million dollars. His smiling face was splashed everywhere. When he won the Chinese National Championships without losing a game, he was pretty much ceded the upcoming World Championships.

I didn't have the money to go to these World Tour events, and so did my own mini-tour, winning every U.S. tournament in sight—the Eastern Open, Southern Open, Pacific Coast Open, the Cary Cup, the Arnold Challenge, the Westchester Open, and of course men's singles at the USA Nationals in Las Vegas. It was a good warm-up for the Worlds, and put some change in my pocket—but where Coach Wang was winning millions, I was winning thousands, with first place prize money for these tournaments ranging from one to three thousand dollars each.

The first thing I did with the prize money was send an anonymous bank check to Double Happiness for the stolen

The Spirit of Pong

clothes. I sent another one to the Chinese National Training Center for the broken window. I considered sending one to Satoh, but how does one send a check to a spirit at a location that doesn't even know of his existence?

Chapter 11
Wembley Stadium

The World Championships were to be held at Wembley Stadium in London in April. I could spend hours talking about my training for the Worlds, traveling there, the huge playing hall, the players, and all my easy early-round wins. In the quarterfinals I knocked off world #5, Yan Zhiheng and his incredible serves—only now they were just things to be dissected and analyzed, and soon the Chinese star would have the ignominious nightmare of losing to an American. Next came Bai Hanhui in the semifinals, former world #1, but knocked down to #2 by Coach Wang. My old American rival, Derek Klaus Hsu, had done pretty well to make the final 32 before getting crushed 4-0 by Bai. Maybe he too should train in China? But against me, Bai had incredible quickness and a powerful forehand, but I was quicker and more powerful.

Yes, I could spend hours talking about these matches. But I won't. They were everything. They were nothing.

Because all that mattered was that, inevitably, I would be in the final, facing the new Chinese Champion and world #1, Coach Wang. He'd easily beaten the powerful topspins of world #3 Fang Guiying in the semifinals, beating him four straight games in the time it took him to smoke one cigarette. Coach Wang, the man I had accepted as my coach and knew my game, a player I could never defeat. The stands would be jammed,

The Spirit of Pong

most of them naively screaming for me, the underdog from America.

There was a pre-match press conference. I attended with the USA Men's Team Coach, Dan Steth, a former U.S. champion who'd coached me throughout the tournament, often giving excellent advice between games. We both sat at a small table at the front of the press room, facing a mob of reporters and photographers. I sat on the far left, with Dan at my side toward the middle.

I stared as Coach Wang entered the press room, with the ever-present cigarette in his mouth, which seemed frozen into a smile. He never even glanced at me as he took his seat at the very center of the table, forcing Coach Dan to move over, which forced me more off to the side as well.

Chinese Head Coach Kong Guoliang followed behind Coach Wang, and sat in the vacant right side of the table. At his heels were the Kunming wolfdogs, Ping and Pong on leashes. I couldn't imagine a U.S. player or USA Table Tennis paying to fly in a pair of dogs for the World Championships, but that's the difference between table tennis in the U.S. and China. If Kong wants his dogs, he gets his dogs. Also attending was every news person from every country in the world. Even the U.S. media, with an American in the final, had suddenly realized what an important sport ping-pong was. We faced dozens of news cameras, many of them live.

I answered the usual questions about my hopes (to win), my dreams (to win), and my aspirations (to win). Coach Dan raved about how much I'd improved. Surprisingly, so did Coach Wang—he knew how to work the press.

"He is greatest American player ever," Coach Wang declared, puffing on a cigarette to the horror of many. "He has much to be proud of." He reached over and patted me on the back. "But the journey ends now. No American can beat a Chinese champion. Americans are too soft and weak to compete in a true sport like table tennis." There were gasps from the room, and I could hear the scratching of pens as the news people took notes. Ping the wolfdog growled.

"Are you nuts?" exclaimed Coach Dan.

"What he means is—" began Coach Kong.

The Spirit of Pong

"I meant what I said," Coach Wang said, turning to face Coach Kong.

"Americans are—" began Coach Kong.

"Just shut up," Coach Wang said. "The press are not here for you. They are here for *me*, and perhaps the American. You saw nothing in me until I began to win. I got here without you, and I'll win without you."

He shoved Coach Kong. It wasn't an aggressive shove, not meant to knock Kong off his feet, more a playful, "*You are nothing*" shove to show dominance. But nobody told Ping the wolfdog, who lunged forward and bit Coach Wang on the leg.

"*Ow!*" he cried. Coach Kong grabbed Ping by the collar and pulled him off. Pong began to whimper.

"That is the difference between Chinese champions and American pretenders," said Coach Wang, ignoring the injury. "Chinese champions bite. American pretenders whimper. I am through here." He rose to his feet. Before leaving, he leaned over to me and whispered, "You think I got the world's attention?" Smiling and shaking his head, he threw his cigarette to the floor and left without a limp. Unfortunately, the injury didn't seem severe.

"I apologize for the behavior of our player," said Coach Kong. "He dishonors and shames us. Is it better that a dishonorable Chinese wins, or an honorable American? That is my dilemma." Then, as dozens of press people screamed questions, he leaned over to me and whispered. "Beat him."

I started to respond, but he suddenly went still. So did everyone else in the room, as if frozen in place. There was a tap on my shoulder. I turned, and there stood Ogimura, Rong, and Satoh. Or at least their translucent spirits.

"This brings back memories," said Ogimura, looking about. "This was where I won my first world championship, in this very stadium, in 1954." Then he turned to me. "For this match, you must drink as much of the Sweat of Champions as you are able. You will need every drop."

"You have been through the worst," said Rong. "Nothing more can hurt you."

"Nobody thought I could win either," said Satoh.

All three looked depressed.

The Spirit of Pong

"Do I have a chance?" I asked.

"There's always a chance," said Ogimura. "You must find a way. You might even learn the fourth secret, which cannot be taught."

"What is the fourth secret, Coach Ogi?"

"Find a way," he repeated. Then all three faded out.

"*How?*" I screamed.

"Excuse me?" asked Coach Kong, pulling back from me as if I were a bug. Ping and Pong began barking.

"What do you mean?" cried one of the news people. Everyone was looking at me.

"I think he's wondering how great it is that an American has gotten this far at the Worlds," said Coach Dan.

I left quickly. Find a way? But how?

Chapter 12
The Spirits of Champions

Jan-Ove Waldner, photo by Diego Schaaf

I drank as much of the Sweat of Champions as I could down; for some reason, I never had to use the restroom afterwards as it was all somehow absorbed. I felt incredible, and yet I knew it wouldn't help. Coach Wang also had the Mind, Body, and my own Paddle of Pong, had undoubtedly overdosed on his own Sweat of Champions—and most important, he knew my game. If only I had studied Coach Wang's game more during the short time we had trained together. Would that have helped? I didn't know; the mysterious world of championship table tennis didn't work by ordinary rules.

Coach Dan and I studied videos of Coach Wang. He and I both played similarly, with powerful topspin attacks from both forehand and backhand. I was a bit more forehand-oriented, he more willing to play backhand. He could block against attacks better, while I had better off-table lobbing defense.

"Keep your serve short," Coach Dan said. "Attack his serve when you can, but otherwise drop it short. In the rally move the ball around. Attack his middle and wide forehand.

The Spirit of Pong

Whatever you do, don't get stuck going backhand-to-backhand—that's where he dominates, so change directions quickly to his middle or wide forehand. And watch his shoulders—when he smashes or loop kills he always fakes the other way." He said a lot more and it was all great advice. But it was worthless in this hopeless situation, and so I mostly tuned him out.

The match would be best of seven, with each game to eleven. Soon, gorged with the Sweat of Champions, full of advice from Coach Dan and memories of tactics from Rong, and with Satoh's very own Paddle of Pong, I was out on the table, facing Coach Wang. Coach Dan sat in my corner. Coach Wang was alone other than the perpetual cigarette dancing in the corner of his mouth.

After a week of play, Wembley Stadium smelled like a locker room. The stands were jammed at full capacity, with 90,000 people screaming for action in a sea of red chairs. I looked about the playing court, which was extra-large, with barriers all around, covered with sponsor logos. There were two umpires, one to each side, along with scorekeepers in all four corners, all in uniform with jackets and ties, and matching pants.

There was a VIP section directly behind us. Sitting there were the greats of our sport: past Chinese champions, including Zhang Jike, Ma Long, Wang Liqin, Kong Linghui, Liu Guoliang, Guo Yuehua, Xi Enting, Deng Yaping, Zhang Yining, and others—including perhaps the greatest Chinese star of them all, Kong Guoliang, the snubbed Chinese coach. Also there were past European champions, including Jan-Ove Waldner, Jorgen Persson, Werner Schlager, Jean-Philippe Gatien, Jean-Michel Saive, Istvan Jonyer, Stellan Bengtsson, and others. I caught the eye of the great Waldner, who nodded, and raised his fist in a gesture of support.

I won the choice of serve or receive, and gave Coach Wang the serve. "It won't matter," he muttered with a smile, loud enough for me to hear.

If this were a story, he'd win the first three games, then I'd fight back in dramatic fashion and win in seven. Then I'd be carried off the field as a great American hero. In reality, the first part was true. He didn't just beat me the first three games, he

The Spirit of Pong

pretty much annihilated me. I did everything right, and everything wrong. No matter what I did, he was ready. He didn't just "know my game" in a technical sense; he knew it in a much deeper fashion, in a purely instinctual way. The mysterious world of championship table tennis had made me a champion, but it had also made Coach Wang my insurmountable master.

Between games Coach Dan continued with his great, but useless advice. After an 11-5 drubbing in game one, he'd calmly advised me to move the ball around more so that Coach Wang couldn't anticipate my every move. After an even worse 11-4 second game, he remained calm as he told me the exact same thing in different words. From his point of view, I was playing right into Coach Wang's game, since he was ready for whatever I did. In reality, what choice did I have? After an 11-3 shellacking in game three, Coach Dan became a bit shrill, trying to get through to me how important it was to not be so predictable. He meant well.

"If you don't—" he began. And then, like before at the end of the press conference, he and everyone went still and silent.

"If your opponent knows your game, then you must change your game." I whirled around, and standing behind me in the playing court was the man considered by many the greatest player of all time, Jan-Ove Waldner, the 1989 and 1997 world champion and 1992 Olympic champion from Sweden. I looked over to the VIP section, and Waldner was there as well, frozen in place like the others.

"If you are Waldner, then who is that?" I asked, gesturing to the other very-much-alive Waldner. "Are you his spirit, separate from his body?"

"I am not the spirit of Jan-Ove Waldner," said the slightly translucent figure. "I am the spirit of what made him a champion."

"Won't he miss you?"

"Let's just say that if Waldner plays a match right now, he won't do so well. But let's focus on your game. You're not doing so well."

"He knows my game."

The Spirit of Pong

Waldner shook his head. "The Chinese knew my game as well, but it didn't help them because I constantly changed my game. That's what you must do."

"But I've learned a particular style. How can I learn another one in the middle of a match?"

"You have the Body, Mind, and Paddle of Pong. That allows you to do things you cannot possibly imagine. But only if you try."

"So what do I do?"

"Why not move away from the table and straight-arm loop with sidespin from both sides?" asked a suddenly-appearing spirit-of-what-made-Jonyer-a-champion. That would be Istvan Jonyer, 1975 world men's singles champion. "Like this?"

Suddenly the Hungarian Jonyer was battling on the table with the Czech Anton Stipancic in a ghostly replica of that battle from so long ago. Stipancic mostly stayed close to the table, one of the first players to focus on looping close to the table, but the off-table Jonyer pulled it out, 21-19 in the fifth, back when games were to 21.

"Watch and learn," said Waldner. Then he, Jonyer, and Stipancic faded out.

"—vary your game, you have no chance," finished Coach Dan as the crowd came back to life.

Off-table two-winged straight-arm sidespin looping? That was a style of the past, since modern players stayed closer to the table, only backing up on defense, with shorter strokes rather than the cumbersome, straight-arm looping technique used by some players from the past. But it was worth a shot. I glanced over at the real Jonyer, who like Waldner before, pumped his fist at me. He'd gained weight since his playing days.

Jonyer did a lot of backhand serves, something I never did. I'd spent years perfecting my serves, both before and after my Chinese odyssey, but it had been mostly forehand serves. But what did I have to lose? I opened the fourth game with a backhand serve—and somehow, it came naturally.

I saw Coach Wang hesitate, and make a somewhat timid return. He knew my game, but this was not my game. I followed with a swooping forehand sidespin loop, as I'd seen Jonyer do. Coach Wang blocked it back to my wide forehand. Normally I'd

The Spirit of Pong

have stayed close to the table and looped again, a powerful shot that Coach Wang would be fully ready for. Instead, I stepped back. The ball was well angled, and by stepping back, I had even more ground to cover as the ball shot away from me. Using my Body of Pong speed, I ran it down, way off to my wide forehand, and did a sweeping Jonyer sidespin loop—around the right side of the net!

Where did that come from? I'd done shots like that in practice, for fun, but never in a serious match. The sidespin pulled the ball onto the table, but since it passed the net below net height, it barely bounced on the other side. Coach Wang tried to block it, but the ball shot off to the side.

In the second point I backhand sidespin looped a ball. Coach Wang blocked it, but I swooped in with another Jonyer forehand loop, this time taking the ball near the table and ripping it with speed as well as sidespin, so the ball both sped past Coach Wang and jumped away from him.

"So you are Istvan Jonyer?" asked Coach Wang. "Very smart, but I do not need to know your game to beat an inferior style from the past."

The next point I was again sidespin looping, but Coach Wang quickly forced me off the table. The problem with straight-arm looping is that it's a longer, slower swing, and so the shorter swings of modern table tennis, with the arm more bent, is quicker, and so allows a player to stay at the table, while the slower player is forced off. This gives the player with the quicker stroke time to rip the ball. And rip it Coach Wang did. After two points like this, the score was back to even, 2-2.

"You need to be quicker and fast," said the Spirit of Zhuang Zedong, the world champion in 1961, 1963, and 1965, who had died in 2013. I realized the hall had grown still and quiet again.

"You want me to switch to pips-out penhold?"

"You want to win?" Suddenly Zhuang was battling on the table with Li Furong, the man he'd defeated in all three finals, though many believed the latter had been ordered to dump. Both played similar close-to-table pips-out penhold styles, blocking and smashing everything off the bounce with both backhand and forehand. Then they faded out.

The Spirit of Pong

Then it was Mitsuro Kohno, 1977 world champion from Japan, also a quick pips-out penhold player, beating Guo Yuehua in the final. Then they faded out.

Then it was Jiang Jialiang, 1985 and 1987 champion from China, another quick pips-out penhold player, battling in the 1987 final with Waldner. I watched as, up 2-1 in games, he came back from down 16-20 in that famous fourth game to reach 20-20, and then walked around the table pumping his fist in the air. He went on to win the game and championships, 24-22 over a shaken Waldner. Then they faded out.

Then it was Liu Guoliang, 1999 world champion and 1996 Olympic champion from China, another quick pips-out penhold player with devastating serves, who sometimes used the inverted side on the back of his racket, defeating teammate and penhold looper Ma Lin in the final. Then they faded out and the roar of the crowd returned.

And so I gave it a try.

"You've got to be kidding," said Coach Wang. The crowd had also gasped when I'd served penhold style with a suddenly pips-out penhold racket. Wang had attacked the serve to my backhand; I quick-blocked it back, and then stepped around and flat-killed the ball with my forehand. All with the penhold grip, with the racket upside down, like holding chopsticks. Somehow the grip seemed natural.

"Zhuang Zedong says hello," I said.

Coach Wang approached the umpire. "He's illegally changed rackets." It's not legal to change rackets in the middle of a match, unless it is accidentally broken, and then it must be replaced by one that is of the same type.

Before the umpire could ask, I handed over the racket, which had already switched back to a smooth inverted shakehands racket. I'd been through this already in previous matches.

"Looks the same to me," said the umpire.

"Very good," said Coach Wang. "But how long do you think it will take me to adapt to this new but also flawed style?"

"How many styles are there?"

As soon as play began again, the racket went back to pips-out. But the Zhuang style only worked for two points; the

The Spirit of Pong

next point afterwards Coach Wang pinned me to the backhand with a loop, and then ripped a winner to my wide forehand. The problem with the style in the modern game is that it focused on blocking, allowing the opponent to play a big topspin game. Jammed at the table, the blocker didn't have time to react. And so I could only watch as Coach Wang ripped the winner.

There were many more styles. After visits from Guo Yuehua, 1983 and 1985 world champion from China, Xi Enting, 1973 world champion from China, Seiji Ono, 1979 world champion from Japan, Yoo Nam Kyu, 1988 Olympic champion from South Korea, Ryu Seung Min, 2004 Olympic champion from South Korea—with perhaps the fastest feet of all time—and Ma Lin, 2008 Olympic champion from China, I was an all-forehand penhold looper, running all over the court and playing nearly all forehand topspin attack, sometimes playing lefty like Yoo.

Then I chopped and looped after visits from chopper-loopers Joo Sehyuk of South Korea, 2003 world finalist, Liang Geliang of China, semifinalist in 1977 and 1979, and Chen Xinhua, 1985 world cup champion from China. I switched hands and played lefty again, looping forehands off the bounce for winners after a visit from Jean-Philippe Gatien, the incredibly quick 1993 world champion from France. I curled my index finger around the edge of the blade and dropped balls short and attacked from both wings after a visit from the short but deadly Stellan Bengtsson, 1971 world champion from Sweden who was trained in Japan for three and a half months by Ogimura. I kept my finger curled around the edge of the blade and used the powerful forehand loop and backhand smash of Jorgen Persson, the tall 1991 world champion, after his visit. I played close to the table with long pips with sponge on one side, inverted on the other, flipping the racket constantly, after a visit from three-time English champion Carl Prean.

I put my finger down the middle of my racket and acrobatically lobbed and looped after a visit from Nobuhiko Hasegawa, the 1967 world champion from Japan, and did the same with a more normal shakehands grip after visits from other stars like former world #1 and 1993 world finalist Jean-Michel Saive of Belgium, and 1968 European champion Dragutin

The Spirit of Pong

Surbek of Yugoslavia. I went back to penhold and looped and smashed relentlessly after a visit from Shigeo Itoh, 1969 world champion from Japan. I combined shakehands attack and control after another visit from Waldner and Kong Linghui, the 1995 champion and 2000 Olympic champion from China.

I switched back to penhold with inverted, and topspinned from both sides, using the reverse side of my racket for backhands rather than the traditional way, after a visit from Wang Hao, 2009 world champion from China. I switched back to shakehand and continued topspinning from both sides, with an especially powerful backhand loop, after a visit from Werner Schlager, 2003 world champion from Austria. And then I was an all-out two-winged looper, effortlessly ripping winners from both sides while staying near the table, after visits from Ma Long, 2015 world champion, and Zhang Jike, 2011 and 2013 world champion and 2012 Olympic champion, both from China.

I felt like Mr. Scrooge, with all these spirits dropping by. One by one they visited, showed me their style. All wanted me to defeat Coach Wang.

Each style worked for a few points, and then I'd have to move on. But point by point, and then game by game, as the frenzied crowd watched in amazement, I worked my way back into the match. Soon it was 3-3, and we were into the seventh and final game.

After I won the fourth game, Coach Dan had said, "When I said to vary your game, I didn't mean that much!" After the fifth game he'd said, "What the heck is going on?" After the sixth game, he'd just grinned, shrugged his shoulders, and said, "I have no idea what you're doing, but just keep doing it."

But I was running out of styles. I'd played every style used by every modern men's champion. I'd even played one point as Satoh. I'd lost that point since what had worked for him against hardbat simply didn't work against modern sponge, and Coach Wang had easily ripped a winner. I'd won two points each as Ogimura and Rong after visits from them.

I dug in deep as more champions visited. There were the lefty off-table topspinners Appelgren of Sweden, former world #1 and 1983 world cup champion, and Jacques Secrétin, 1976 European champion from France. The big backhand looping of

The Spirit of Pong

Andzej Grubba of Poland, 1988 World Cup Champion, and Jorg Rosskopf of Germany, 1998 world cup champion. The Seemiller grips of the American stars Dan Seemiller, five-time U.S. Champion, and Eric Boggan, two-time U.S. Champion and top twenty in the world, both of whom used only one side of the paddle for both forehand and backhand, switching between inverted and antispin.

And then it was 9-all in the seventh.

Chapter 13
Match Point   **Marty Reisman, photo by Mal Anderson**

"I've been keeping track," said Coach Wang. "You've gone through every style used by every modern champion. All that are left are pale imitations, styles that can't compete, even for a point. What will you do now?"

It was a good question. At 8-8 I'd won a point with a Seemiller anti-spin drop shot followed by a big forehand, but up 9-8, he'd ripped a winner off my anti shot. What next?

"Time!" said the umpire. I was taking too much time between shots.

The Spirit of Pong

"Time out!" yelled Coach Dan. This gave me one minute to think things over. I walked over to Dan's corner.

"I don't know what forces are at work here," said Coach Dan, "and I really don't want to know what's going on. But whatever it is, keep doing it. That's all I can say."

I nodded, but I still didn't know what to do. Then Dan froze and the hall went quiet.

"Try hardbat," said the spirit of Marty Reisman, two-time U.S. champion and the one many thought might have won the Worlds in 1952 if not for Satoh. The flamboyant American star had died in 2012, but not before winning the U.S. Hardbat Championships in 1997 at age 67.

If this were a fable, I would use hardbat, win the next two points, and I'd be champion. But *hardbat*?

"What have you got to lose?" asked the spirit of Dick Miles, ten-time U.S. Champion and 1959 semifinalist at the Worlds. He'd died in 2010.

Standing behind them were a crowd of others—five-time world champion Viktor Barna of Hungary, known for his backhand flip kill; four-time world champion Richard Bergmann of Austria and England, and two-time champion Johnny Leach of England, both known for their backspin defense; two-time world champion Bohumil Váňa of Czechoslovakia, who hopped when he hit his incredibly steady forehand; Ferenc Sido of Hungary, who could equally attack or defend, the last hardbat player to win the Worlds in 1953, and who, against all odds and against sponge players, would make the final again in 1959, where he would lose to . . . Rong Guotuan. And many more.

I had no other options. I was serving at the end. I considered using one of the famous Sol Schiff fingerspins from the 1930, where you spin the ball with your fingers, but they were illegal, and I'd likely be faulted the point. I'd play it clean.

I served, and I could see Coach Wang's eyes go wide as he realized I was now using a hardbat. Even the umpires leaned forward as the sound of a hardbat is distinctive. He pushed my serve back. I did a Barna backhand flip; he counter-hit to my forehand. I snapped in a Reisman forehand, but he blocked it back to my backhand. And suddenly I was off the table, chopping like Bergmann and Leach, but facing topspins they had

The Spirit of Pong

never had to face. But I was used to these topspins, and a hardbat is easy to chop with. Suddenly Coach Wang dropped the ball short. I reacted instantly, and with my Ogimura-trained Body of Pong, I raced forward, and did a Dick Miles-styled windmill-style wind-up forehand smash for a winner.

I led 10-9 championship point.

"*Really?*" asked Coach Wang, shaking his head with a trace of a grin. The umpire called me over to examine my racket, but it had conveniently gone back to inverted again.

Coach Wang and I both knew that old-style hardbat wouldn't work twice. But what was I supposed to do? I had nothing left. I played another hardbat point. Coach Wang attacked my serve, and once again I was off the table chopping. But this time Coach Wang went back and forth between steady topspins and rips, and finally one of my chops went a touch too high, and *wham*! The point was over, and it was 10-10 in the seventh. I had blown my championship point and my chance at glory.

And then, in a repeat of Jiang in 1987, Coach Wang circled the table, pumping his fist in the air. I could only watch.

Chapter 14

The Spirit of Pong

Deng Yaping

"I admire your bravery," said Coach Wang after he completed his circuit. "But once again you have overplayed your hand. You have run out of styles. Or will you try sandpaper next?" He laughed as he stood at the table, preparing to serve.

He was right. Hardbat was definitely out. There was nothing left for me. I stalled as long as I could, but when the umpire waved for me to continue for the third time and started to stand up, I knew I was out of time. In desperation, I brought back Jonyer style. It led to a nice counterlooping duel, but inevitably Coach Wang's more modern loop over-powered my off-table sidespinning ones, which had only worked when he'd been caught off guard.

I was down 10-11 match and championship point.

"There is nothing left for you here except to go back to America, defeated. No American can ever beat a Chinese champion, and no one—"

And then he and Wembley Stadium once again went still and silent. Coach Wang was left with his mouth half open.

"How come I'm the only woman spirit you've met?" asked the very short and slightly translucent Deng Yaping. I stared down in awe at the greatest woman player ever—three-time World Champion and two-time Olympic gold medalist in women's singles, and #1 in the world for pretty much the entire

The Spirit of Pong

1990s. As if that weren't enough, after her playing career she'd gotten a Ph.D in Land Economy from the University of Cambridge.

"I've been wondering the same thing," I said. I was no longer shocked by the appearance of another legend. "I haven't exactly been sending out invitations. They just keep dropping in. But they've been very helpful."

"Half the world titles have been won by women," Deng said. "Your own country has never won a men's singles title, but your Ruth Aarons won women's singles twice. Whoever's sending out those invitations better get on the ball. And may I ask why you are only doing men's styles? There are a lot of women champions, and we have our own styles!"

Oops. I hadn't even thought of that. I'd always studied the men's game, but had neglected studying the women.

"You're right. Sorry about that. Should I copy your style, Miss Deng?" She'd played with inverted on the forehand, and long pips with sponge on the backhand—but unlike most others with that combination, she could attack with the pips, which weren't quite as long as conventional long pips and were really medium-long pips. She stayed close to the table with one of the quickest, most ferocious attacks ever.

"That won't be necessary, and I'm not Deng Yaping, she's over there." She pointed at the real one, who was in mid-clap in the VIP section. "And it's Dr. Deng. But you can call me Deng. Like the others, I'm the spirit of what made her a champion. But in this case, I'm a whole lot more."

"How?"

"What you face is insignificant compared to what others have faced through the years. Win three points just so you can win a title? How does that compare with, say, the struggles of Rong Guotuan?"

It didn't.

"When I was first on the Chinese National Team, they decided I was too short to ever be a champion. And so I was sent home. I had to work harder than anyone, both to overcome my size, *and* to prove to others I'd overcome my size problem. All champions have something to overcome, and if they don't, they never learn the fourth and final secret to table tennis."

The Spirit of Pong

"There's a fourth?" I asked. "I thought there was just the Body, Mind, and Paddle of Pong?"

"That's what Coach Wang believes, and that's why he can never be a Champion, even if he were to win this one title. I'm here to teach you that final secret. A true champion has one more quality, one that can allow him to defeat *anyone*. The Spirit of Pong."

Suddenly I saw light at the end of the ping-pong table, a way to win these last few points. But what was spirit? All the spirit in the world couldn't overcome Coach Wang's mastery over me. Could it?

"I'm ready to learn," I said. Would this mean spending a year with Deng, like I'd done with Ogimura and Rong, to earn the Spirit of Pong? But it would be rather funny, leaving Coach Wang with his mouth gaping like that for a full year. Perhaps I'd stuff earthworms in it.

"No matter what happens, no matter how bad it gets, no matter how things seem, believe in yourself and give an all-out effort. If you do all that, the impossible becomes possible. Even a shrimp like me, or an American, can become the best."

"So, basically, you are saying to have confidence and try my best."

"That's it. That is the secret of Champions, in every sport, and in all other endeavors. It cannot be taught, it can only be learned."

I took a deep breath. "And how do I earn the Spirit of Pong?"

"You don't *earn it*," she said. "You *do it*." And then she faded out.

"—ever will," finished Coach Wang. The sounds of Wembley Stadium returned. "There's nothing left for you here."

I looked up at him for a moment, then looked away. He was nothing; destiny was in my hands, not his. But what was my destiny? Was it all going to end this next point?

Perhaps not, but this next point was all that mattered *now*. A champion has to focus; both Rong and Ogimura had harped on that. Nothing in the universe mattered except this next point, and then the point after that, and so on until the match was over. No, that was also wrong; nothing in the

The Spirit of Pong

universe mattered except *this next shot*. And then the one after that. And so on. Each deserved the same all-out effort, just as Deng had said.

But how should I play? Hardbat was out; so were all the many styles and rackets I'd used, to limited success.

"So what'll it be?" Coach Wang asked. "I can beat any style you copy."

Then it hit me—she'd said to believe in myself.

Believe in myself and give an all-out effort. *That* was the Spirit of Pong. To believe in myself I had to be myself, not Jonyer, Waldner, Ma Long, or anyone else. Just me, fighting as hard as I could with the tools that I had.

There was something new here, something I hadn't felt before. I'd always tried my best, or thought I had. But now my muscles were tingling; the Body of Pong. The mind was alert; the Mind of Pong. The aura around my Paddle of Pong suddenly blazed like a torch, a bonfire to the dim firefly-like aura of Coach Wang's Paddle of Pong. I barely noticed the gasp from the crowd, but I did see the sudden hesitation from Coach Wang, who was getting ready to receive my serve. I had the Body, Mind, and Paddle of Pong, and now I had the Spirit of Pong.

I faked heavy backspin but serve no-spin, short to the middle. Coach Wang saw it and wasn't fooled. He reached in to flip aggressively to my wide forehand. I no longer needed to channel Guo Yuehua or Zhang Jike or any of the others; *I* was ready for it. Just me.

At the last second he stopped his flip and dropped the ball short to my backhand, completely catching me off guard. I fought to get to it, but I'd over-reacted to his expected attack to the forehand, and was way too far to my right. At the last second, I lunged, and just hit the ball off the tip of my racket.

The ball rose—too high, an easy kill for Coach Wang. I saw his eyes go wide as he set up for the shot. There was no physical way to cover both wide corners; all I could do was guess and hope.

Everything went into slow motion. Which way would he go? If I guessed, it'd be 50-50, and even if I guessed right I'd still be in trouble.

The Spirit of Pong

In an instant I saw what I'd seen, but hadn't noticed. When he smashed to the forehand, he always brought his shoulders back farther than usual, making it look like he was smashing to my backhand. When he smashed to the backhand, he minimized the rotation, making it look like he was going to the forehand, and then at the last second would bring his shoulders back. Coach Dan had pointed this out before the match, but I hadn't paid attention, thinking I had no chance.

He brought his shoulders back farther than usual, as if setting up to smash to my backhand. As he hit the ball, I moved to my right, my forehand, and that's where he smashed.

Believe. All-out effort.

I counter-smashed a winner.

11-all.

I stared at Coach Wang, and he stared back. I'd like to say that he looked away, afraid, but all I saw was determination. I was going to have to earn this.

He prepared to serve. And that's when I saw it, the slight bulge in his cheek. I thought back, and flashed back to his past serves—sure enough, there was that same bulge when he was about to serve fast and deep. He was tensing up to serve long, like the player I'd played long ago who stuck out his tongue. But to the forehand or backhand?

As he served my muscles tensed and I prepared to move sideways. Knowing it wouldn't go short simplified things. The instant I saw the ball coming off his racket—to my backhand—I was off, stepping around to use my forehand.

Believe. All-out effort.

I ripped the serve with perhaps the most powerful loop I'd ever done, right down the line to his forehand. Coach Wang could only watch it go by.

12-11 championship point. I would again serve for the match and the championship. I looked over at Coach Wang, and he was staring at me. The grin was gone, replaced by a look of absolute hatred.

Anger can lead a person into mistakes. It can also lead them to herculean effort.

I didn't want to risk a long serve, and my previous serve had been no-spin, and he'd flipped it with ease. I served heavy

The Spirit of Pong

backspin, short to the forehand. This meant I'd have to guard the wide forehand, leaving my backhand side somewhat open. But I hadn't done this serve in a while, so it was time.

Rather than attack it, he again dropped it short. I stepped in and backhand flipped with heavy topspin to his deep backhand. But he'd somehow anticipated this, and was already there, ready with a big forehand loop to my wide backhand. I blocked down the line to his forehand. But Coach Wang was ready with an off-the-bounce forehand counterloop to my wide forehand, unreachable. Or was it?

There's a story of a small woman who saw a car run over her baby, pinning its legs to the ground. The woman, filled with adrenaline, lifted the car off her baby, and the baby was saved. Later, she was unable to even budge the car. That was me. Complete effort and beyond was needed, and so the muscles screamed but did the impossible, and I was there, with a powerful forehand counterloop. And so began the counterlooping duel for the ages.

I could not miss, but neither could Coach Wang. Back and forth we ripped the ball, shot after shot, heavy topspin to heavy topspin, each of us racing about to forehand loop from all parts of the court. We counterlooped sixty in a row, thirty each, throwing our bodies into each shot.

And then his ball came too low, and nicked the net on my wide forehand side and began to dribble over. Instantly I lunged forward. But the ball hit the side edge, and bounced sideways, away from me, slowly moving away and dropping toward the floor. It seemed in slow motion, slow enough that it seemed to freeze in mid-air as I watched. Championships have been decided this way. In 1973, Xi Enting, leading 19-18 in the fifth, won with a net and an edge over Kjell Johansson. Like Johansson, I could only watch the unreturnable shot.

That's when the Spirit of Pong completely overcame me.

My legs exploded, and suddenly I was there, stretched out. I just reached the ball, and sidespin looped it *around* the net, like Jonyer, but this time it was *me*. Coach Wang's eyes went wide again as he moved toward the ball, but all he could do was make a lunging block. The ball came back to me, slightly high.

Believe. All-out effort.

The Spirit of Pong

I smashed the ball past the shocked eyes of Coach Wang before he could even react. His cigarette fell from his mouth as the ball shot past him, and off into the court where it bounced a few times and came to a stop against the barriers, a small, insignificant ball and the most important object in the universe.

The crowd exploded. Coach Dan and my teammates sprinted onto the court, even Derek Klaus Hsu. They carried me off the court.

I had captured the whale.

THE END

The Spirit of Pong

Bonus Story:
Ping-Pong Ambition
By Larry Hodges

Toby, shrunk down to one half inch tall, screamed and banged his fists on the rounded white walls of his prison. From outside he could hear the fading laughter of the genie that had imprisoned him in the ping-pong ball. How could this have happened?

All he'd wanted was to be the greatest ping-pong player ever. He'd been practicing on his table tennis robot, smacking in ball after ball, when the ball had broken, and out of it had come a wrinkled old genie.

"I have been trapped in that ping-pong ball for ten thousand years," cried the genie. "For freeing me, I grant you one wish."

He'd made his wish, but had been met with treachery. And now he was stuck in that very same ball, the crack mended, just himself and the thick, red book the genie had given him. He let loose another set of screams.

When he finally calmed down, he sat cross-legged on the celluloid floor and sobbed quietly to himself for a time. Then he opened the book, *Magic of the Djinn*. It was the fattest book he'd ever seen, as wide as his index finger was tall, probably over a thousand pages long of seemingly normal paper—but paging to the back, he saw that it somehow contained ten million pages. He began to read, starting in the A's.

He read about Abominable Snowmen, the making of, and decided to try the spell. He created one, right there in the ping-pong ball. The creature roughed him up, but fortunately it

The Spirit of Pong

tired before killing him, and he was able to read ahead and learn about Amulets for protection.

Then he was on to learning about Adepts, the Alexandrian Path of Witchcraft, Antipathetic Magic, and much more.

The first few hundred years were tedious. Often he'd throw down the book and attack the walls with every spell he'd learned so far. But nothing could break through, not even Astrology or Aztec Magic. His powers ended at the walls of the ping-pong ball.

Finally, after four hundred years, he reached the B's, and learned how to handle Boredom. As he continued to develop his powers, life became more comfortable. He furnished his prison alphabetically with all the comforts of home.

As the eons went by his skin became wrinkled and gray, and his dark hair turned white and fell out. He decided his age was a badge of honor, and so did not use the Beautification spells he had learned. He still felt young on the inside.

It took him five thousand years to reach the P's, and there he learned all the magic needed for Ping-Pong. He created his own ping-pong table, net, rackets and balls. By folding the far side of the ping-pong table to vertical, he could play against the rebounds and rally by himself. He spent many a happy afternoon practicing over the next thousand years. Then he got to the R's and T's, and created his own Table Tennis Robot, and from there on he split his time between the robot and the book.

At the rate of one thousand pages per year, a little less than three pages per day, he slowly worked his way through all the magic in the book. Finally, after ten thousand years, he put the book down for the last time, having mastered the intricacies of zombies. He now had all the powers of a genie and five thousand years of table tennis practice. And yet he was still a prisoner.

Then he heard a sound from outside. He put his ear against the wall, and there was no question about it. It was the sound of ping-pong.

Suddenly his world turned upside down, throwing him off his feet. His ping-pong table barely missed crashing into him.

The Spirit of Pong

Something smashed into the side of his ping-pong prison, slamming him against the wall. His world spun about.

Again something smashed into his prison, and again he and the ball's contents slammed against the wall. It happened over and over and over. Someone outside was playing ping-pong, with Toby's prison as the ball.

There was a sudden screeching sound. His ball had cracked! It was only a slit, but that was all he needed. Grasping the book, he turned himself into Smoke—he'd learned that in the S's—and escaped through the thin gap. Outside he solidified himself at full size. Finally, after ten thousand years, he was *free*!

A man holding a ping-pong paddle was staring at him. Toby stared back, and then fought back disbelief. Could it be? The man had been playing ping-pong with a robot, just as Toby had done for so many years, and he still had his hair.

"I have been trapped in that ping-pong ball for ten thousand years," Toby finally said, remembering those words from so long ago. "For freeing me, I grant you one wish."

The man was hyper-ventilating, a reasonable reaction when a genie suddenly appears out of a ping-pong ball. Finally he caught his breath.

"Well," said the man, "what I really want is to be the greatest ping-pong player ever." Yes, Toby thought, and boy are you going to regret not wishing for just that!

"But that would be a waste," the man continued. "I can wish for anything, right?"

"Anything in my power," Toby said, "and just about anything *is* in my power."

"Then," the man said, a huge grin on his face, "I wish to have all the powers of a genie. Then I can wish to be the greatest ping-pong player ever, and still have *more* wishes!"

Toby couldn't hold it back any longer, and began to laugh. Ten thousand years of frustration now came out in relieved laughter as the man looked at him in surprise, just as he himself had done so ten thousand years before.

"You *will* have the powers of a genie," Toby finally said between giggles. He handed the book to the man. "It'll take you ten thousand years to learn, so study well!" He pointed a finger

The Spirit of Pong

at his younger self, turning him to Smoke, and with a gesture moved him into the cracked ping-pong ball.

He sealed the crack, put an impervious spell on the walls, and transported it ten thousand years into the past so that it would reappear here at the end of that time. Then he eyed the ping-pong table. With thousands of years of practice, he wouldn't even need to use magic to be the greatest ping-pong player ever.

About the Author

Larry Hodges, of Germantown, MD, is a member of the U.S. Table Tennis Hall of Fame as a coach and writer. He's certified as a National Coach by USA Table Tennis, the highest level, and coaches at the Maryland Table Tennis Center. As a writer he has nine books and over 1500 published articles in over 140 publications. He also does a daily table tennis blog.

He's also an active member of Science Fiction Writers of America, with over 70 short story sales and the novel "Sorcerers in Space," a humorous fantasy about the U.S.-Soviet space race in the 1960s, with sorcerers instead of astronauts. Many of his best stories are compiled in the anthology "Pings and Pongs." His story "The Awakening" was the unanimous grand prize winner at the 2010 Garden State Horror Writers Short Story Competition. His story "Rationalized" won the November 2011 Story Quest Competition.

Visit his science fiction & fantasy page at:
LarryHodges.org
Visit his table tennis page (with links to his other books) and daily blog at:
TableTennisCoaching.com

The Spirit of Pong

Books by Larry Hodges

Table Tennis Tactics for Thinkers

Table Tennis Tips

Table Tennis Tales & Techniques

Professional Table Tennis Coaches Handbook

Table Tennis: Steps to Success

Instructor's Guide to Table Tennis

Sorcerers in Space

The Spirit of Pong

Pings and Pongs

Made in the USA
Middletown, DE
03 October 2016